Praise for From Rubble To Champagne!

"From Rubble To Champagne" is the remarkable story of Vivianne Knebel. From a lonely childhood in ravaged, post WWII Berlin, to young adulthood as part of a wave of struggling German immigrants in Canada, to marriage, family and ultimate fulfillment in the United States, Vivianne's mindful and insightful journey moves and inspires the reader. From Rubble to Champagne is a woman's celebration of challenges overcome and a life fully lived.
—Stephen Metcalfe, Author of The Tragic Age and The Practical Navigator

Ms Knebel's spell binding book is a first hand account of something most of us in the US haven't been exposed to and can't fathom. There are many heart wrenching German Holocaust stories. A story that hasn't been told though is, with post WWII Germany in ruins, the horrific challenges that everyday citizens and families face and how one young girl deals with them. It demonstrates what the human spirit can accomplish when challenged in unfathomable ways.
—Tom Gegax Author, Winning in the Game of Life and The Big Book of Small Business.

The autobiography entitled "From Rubble To Champagne" draws the reader into a riveting account of the author's life story of triumph over tragedy. Vivianne transports you to her early life surviving the horrors of war in Hitler's Nazi Germany. Her indomitable spirit of optimism and perseverance are evident throughout her story and should serve as inspiration for anyone who feels defeated and suppressed. The author tells her life story with grace, charm, and wit. It is a must read for contemporary readers who wish to draw life lessons from our past.
Susan Stuart, M.D.
Board certified top Dermatologist

From Rubble To Champagne

From Rubble To Champagne

Rising From The Ashes Of Wartorn Berlin To A Life Of Grace, Beauty And Gratitude

Vivianne Knebel

Copyright © 2020 Vivianne Knebel
All rights reserved
First Edition

PAGE PUBLISHING, INC.
Conneaut Lake, PA

First originally published by Page Publishing 2020

ISBN 978-1-64701-704-0 (hc)
ISBN 978-1-64701-703-3 (digital)

Printed in the United States of America

To my mother, Marija, who gave me life and endless compassion.

To Wiland, my husband and mentor, with whom I have fallen in love time and time again. I will continue to do so for the rest of my days.

To my children, Nikolai and Tanya, who fill my heart.

Contents

Foreword 11
Preface 15
  1 An Illegitimate Child in Nazi Germany ... 19
  2 A Childhood among the Rubble 38
  3 In the Land of Milk and Honey 71
  4 Love 99
  5 Marriage, Motherhood, and Our
     American Dream 120
  6 Coming into My Own 147
  7 The Most Beautiful Time of My Life 170
Epilogue 193

Foreword

$\mathcal{V}$ivianne Knebel's From *Rubble to Champagne* is not just a poignant autobiography but lays the groundwork for us to reflect on our own lives. Her authenticity and vulnerability magnifies the full range of life's emotions from heartbreak to joyfulness and peace of mind. The reader is the beneficiary of her insights, wisdom and lessons learned throughout her life.

Vivianne was dealt a really tough hand until her later teenage years. It is unlikely that any of us have had to suffer the consequences of the impact of being an illegitimate child and never knowing one's father, growing up in the rubble of a war-torn city, being academically challenged, feeling inferior to one's older sibling and having a free spirited, non-conformist mother. Her life experiences also remind us of the catastrophic collateral consequences of war; its effects for generations on those not reflected in the casualty statistics. The story of how Vivianne survived and ultimately prospered is enough reason to read this beautiful book. I was very inspired when reading how she successfully overcame these life challenges by her capacity to see and appreciate beauty, her perseverance and determination, and her deep sense of gratitude.

This book would also be a wonderful read for those who appreciate a beautiful love story. After almost two decades of a desperate existence, a serendipitous encounter led to a life changing event. Vivianne met and subsequently married Wiland Knebel when she was 21 and for over 54 years they have been each other's biggest cheerleader; together they made their life's dreams a reality.

I would be remiss if I didn't highlight what for me was the most powerful message of this book. It serves as a mirror to our souls, reminding us that all of our lives encompass trying moments and difficult times. It encourages us to reflect on the unique and powerful qualities that have helped us survive and prosper. In so doing it gives us strength and hope for what the future may hold.

On a personal note, my wife and I have been friends with Vivianne and Wiland for over two decades and, on several occasions, have had the good fortune of being guests at their dinner parties. Wonderful hosts but, above all, is Vivianne's talent for creating beauty—from her breathtaking gardens, to their exquisite home and the preparation and presentation of her amazing cuisine. It is all done with a graceful ease that envelopes their guests. And the nourishment is not simply visual and palate pleasing; it stimulates our mind and higher senses.

This book serves as a reminder of the power of gratitude for those who have made an important difference in our lives and for all the blessings, large and small, along our life's journey. Vivianne, thank you for your gift of *From Rubble to Champagne*. It has enriched my life as I am sure it will many others.

—Walter Green, Author of *This Is The Moment… How One Man's Yearlong Journey Captured the Power of Extraordinary Gratitude*

PREFACE

*M*y desire to write this book began with a prayer. A few years ago, Karin Chevrotée, a dear friend, wrote me a letter that included the following invocation:

> Prayer of Gratitude
>
> Gratitude for the masters I have
>   met along the way,
> Gratitude for life that is ruthless
>   and totally compassionate at
>   the same time,
> Gratitude for being embodied
>   as a human being with the
>   potential to awaken to my
>   ultimate nature,
> Just simple gratitude.
> —Author unknown

As I read these words, I immediately saw the entire arc of my life.

My story began as the illegitimate daughter of a fiercely devoted mother in Berlin, Germany, at the height of Nazi power. After Germany's defeat and the end of World War II, I grew up among rubble, constantly battling hunger and low self-esteem. As a young child, I watched the division of my home city into West Berlin and her brutish sister, East Berlin. As a teenager, I immigrated across the Atlantic to Canada in search of hope and opportunities. But there too I was met with desperate times and had to beg for money for food. I dropped out of school and found employment but with my jobs came numerous instances of sexual harassment. Spiraling downward into depression, I attempted to take my life, but miraculously, a six-year-old child saved me at the very last moment. Shortly thereafter, the pendulum swung from sadness and desperation to happiness and optimism when I met the love of my life, Wiland Knebel. Like me, he was a German immigrant and a child of the war. We built a life together, welcoming two children in the early years of our marriage. We then immigrated again, this time, to the United States, where Wiland found great success in his career and made smart investments. As he made these strides, he inspired me to take risks, embrace new challenges, and to grow. With his encouragement, I learned to pilot a plane, ran a marathon, and tended to a garden that has been featured on an exclusive garden tour. As we have aged, Wiland and I have had to overcome health challenges; I survived breast cancer, and he had major heart surgery. Despite the hardship that illness brings, it has spurred in me a deep desire to embrace a spiritual life and to explore philosophies that enrich my soul. Throughout my journey, I have been blessed to have encountered several individuals who have offered me their helping hands, enabling me to overcome obstacles and to arrive where I am today.

My life has been one of both hardship and comfort, demoralization and fulfillment, searching and finding, and uncertainty and hope. I have learned to embrace life's trials the same way I welcome its joys: both have the capacity to instruct us, to bring us new levels of appreciation, to deepen our understanding of ourselves and the world around us, and to drive us to become our best selves. Reflecting back upon the prayer Karin shared with me, I can say without hesitation that I am truly grateful for it all.

1

AN ILLEGITIMATE CHILD IN NAZI GERMANY

Year 1943–1945

I was born on May 13, 1943, in Berlin, the heart of Nazi Germany. Scarlet banners bearing black swastikas hung throughout the city. The Gestapo, the Nazi party's secret police, ransacked apartments, searching for any Jews who still remained. Military officers and civilians alike greeted each other with raised arms and confident cries of "Heil, Hitler." Ninety percent of the nation's children had joined Hitler Youth—a stream of propaganda proclaiming the virtues of Nazi ideology constantly played over the radio.

I was born in a hospital in Schöneberg, a locality of Berlin. As my mother recovered from her labor, a nurse brought me to her bedside, wrinkling her nose and haughtily proclaiming, "To whom does this little witch belong?" Mama became so livid that she had to restrain herself from punching the nurse in the nose. The insult, however, was not one that surprised my mother. The Reich had indoctrinated the German people with the notion that women should be modest, dedicated to their husbands, and devoted to a Nazified form of Christianity. Mama, by contrast, was an unmarried woman with two daughters by two different men and little interest in religion. Whereas most German mothers chose standard German names like Helga and Ursula for their daughters, Mama rebelliously gave me a French name Vivianne, which means "full of life." Perhaps she knew that I would need a strong and vibrant name to sustain me through the tumult that inevitably lay ahead for an illegitimate child. But this choice would prove challenging for me because Germans looked down upon anything foreign with disdain. Without a father to pass on a surname to me, I was given my mother's Pavić. It was a foreign name, as well.

My mother, Marija Pavić, was born on September 11, 1911, in Berlin. Her father, Georg Pavić, was an immigrant from Srbobran, a town in present-day Serbia. As a young man, Georg worked in Berlin as a hairdresser. Over time, he became quite renowned for his skill and flair. He started entering hairstyling competitions through which he met Elfriede Heisig, a blond-haired, blue-eyed beauty. She hailed from the city of Breslau, which was still under the auspices of Germany at the time. It is currently part of Poland and is now known as Wrocław. After Georg took first prize in a competition with Elfriede as his model and muse, they married. A savvy business-man, Georg eventually came to own three hair salons in Berlin, a hotel on the Baltic Sea, and several holdings in paper. His prosperity enabled him and Elfriede to raise their four children with comfortable surroundings and hired help.

Hitler's rise brought an end to Georg's good fortune. Although he had lived in Germany for years, the Nazi party held his foreign birth against him and stripped him of his businesses and holdings. His only son, Nikolaus, was conscripted into the *Wehrmacht*, the unified armed forces of the Reich. Nikolaus had a close relationship with Marija and often sent her cards from the front. Whenever he wrote, he always included a request for cigarettes. He kept the cigarettes she sent in a cigarette case on which he had scratched his initials. During a battle against the Russian army, a Soviet tank driver discovered the foxhole in which Nikolaus had positioned himself. The driver ran over the foxhole again and again until Nikolaus was buried alive. He was thirty-one years old. The cigarette case was all that survived his horrific death.

Georg contracted liver cancer in the early 1940s and died shortly before I was born. As he lay on his deathbed, he confided in his second daughter, Theodora, "I am worried about Marija." Georg was right to be concerned about her. My mother had chosen a difficult path for herself. Although Georg and Elfriede had maintained a fairly strict household with traditional values, Marija was a free spirit by nature. A striking woman with raven hair and sparkling blue eyes, Marija's delightful sense of humor and warm personality made her irresistible to the men around her. She chose to socialize in diplomatic circles, longing for a connection to the world beyond Germany.

One man in particular captured her heart, Valentino, an attaché at the Spanish embassy. For eight years, Marija maintained a passionate love affair with him, even becoming his fiancée. They were one of the most glamorous couples in Berlin society in their day. But Valentino was eager to climb the ranks within his embassy, and he knew that a German-born woman, who followed her whims and rebelled against traditional norms, would not help him in pursuing his ambition. He reconnected with his childhood sweetheart, who was more capable of conforming to the role expected of a diplomat's wife, and married her. Valentino was promoted to consul.

Heartbroken, Marija flung herself into short-term affairs. She lived in the moment, allowing herself to indulge in whatever suited her fancy without worrying about the consequences. All around her, more and more men were disappearing to the front, and the war was continuing to escalate. As she later explained, "At that time, you didn't know if you were going to live tomorrow," and so she lived as if the present was all that mattered.

A brief relationship with a Yugoslavian courier named Vladimir Pushkevic led to her first pregnancy. Although Vladimir did not marry her when she discovered her condition, or even remain in her life, Marija truly wanted her baby.

She had no qualms about Nazi taboos on having a child out of wedlock. She was proud to become a mother. Yvonne was born on January 25, 1941. Marija immediately adored her.

Motherhood did not stop Marija from seeking new relationships with men. On a fateful evening out at a nightclub, a new suitor emerged. Upon observing her at her table, Dr. Sandor Vargas was so taken by her beauty that he purchased a bouquet of red roses and had them delivered to her on the spot. Attached to the flowers was his business card and the inquiry, "To whom have I sent these flowers?"

Sandor was a cultured and educated Hungarian who played the piano and, according to Marija, had a fine character. He held a doctorate in law from Pázmány Péter Catholic University in Budapest, one of Hungary's oldest and most prestigious institutions of higher education. In January 1941, he was named the prime secretary of the Royal Hungarian Trade Office. In the fall of that year, he received the Collegium

Hungarian Scholarship, through which he traveled to Berlin to study the organization of the German Trade Administration. In late 1942, he returned to his home country and took a job as a foreign trade inspector with the Department of Interstate in the Ministry of Trade and Transport, leaving behind Marija, who was now pregnant with me.

From there, his life is a mystery. There are no further records of him. During my mother's pregnancy, her best friend, Charlotte, traveled to Budapest and managed to see him there. Charlotte told him of my mother's condition, and he assured her that he would take care of us, but my mother never heard from him, and there is no record of him after 1942. I have imagined numerous explanations for his disappearance. Perhaps he viewed his relationship with Mama simply as an affair and wanted nothing more to do with her. Maybe he was among the thirty-eight thousand civilians who died from starvation or military action when Soviet forces laid siege to Budapest in 1944. Maybe he was subjected to Soviet reprisals and taken as a prisoner to Siberia. Or he may have lost his life like millions of others during one of the countless other episodes of violence that took place during the war. Decades later, when I visited Budapest, I pictured him strolling down the same streets where I was walking or drinking a coffee in one of the cafés I passed. I was never able to locate a photo of him but still glanced at the faces of old men across the city, looking for any hint of familiarity or resemblance.

After my mother gave birth to me, she brought me home to an apartment on Wittenbergplatz, a street close to the Berlin Zoo. It was also close to another major Berlin landmark, the *Kaiser-Wilhelm-Gedächtniskirche* or Kaiser Wilhelm Memorial Church, a Protestant Church erected in the 1890s by Kaiser Wilhelm II and named in honor of his grandfather, Kaiser Wilhelm I. The apartment was located in an old and elegant building complete with a commanding flight of marble steps. It had an elaborate iron gate with an imposing porte cochere that led to a cobblestone courtyard. Despite the grandeur that the facade of the building suggested, our accommodations were humble at best. We lived in a small apartment in the back, which in the earlier life of the building was where the servants had resided. Because our apartment did not have a bathtub, we had to go up to the attic to bathe. Mama would have to boil water in big buckets before we could take a bath. We were fortunate enough to have a toilet in our apartment, but in the winter, the water in it often froze, which made it impossible to flush.

The government had assigned Mama this apartment before I was born. She and Yvonne had previously lived in an apartment that Valentino had arranged and paid for, but Allied aircraft had bombed it. The moment the bomb hit, Mama had grabbed Yvonne and sprinted out of the apartment as fast as she could. Yvonne dragged her feet, crying out for the doll she had left behind. But my mother would not allow her to turn back. "You must let it go. You have no choice," she exclaimed to her inconsolable daughter. The apartment was decimated.

During the course of the war, Berlin became the most heavily bombed city in history, with the Allies dropping nearly sixty-eight thousand tons of bombs. When I was six months old, on November 22, 1943, a particularly brutal raid killed 2,000 Berliners and left 175,000 people without a home. The next evening, another bombing caused a thousand people to lose their lives and rendered 100,000 people homeless. Yvonne and I started going to sleep wearing our coats so that if a bomb attack came in the middle of the night, Mama did not have to lose a second dressing us.

One of the bomb shelters we sometimes used was the most famous in Berlin—the *Flakturm Tiergarten* or Zoo flak tower. It was thirteen stories tall and designed with dual offensive and defensive capabilities. Its primary purpose was to serve as a gun platform from which soldiers could shoot down aircrafts and thereby protect government buildings, which were located nearby. Firing from the roof of the tower, Nazi soldiers could take down any plane that came within approximately ten kilometers. The Zoo flak tower also served as a civilian air-raid shelter with a capacity for ten thousand people and even had room for eighty-five hospital beds.

During a bomb attack in 1944, my mother ran toward the Zoo flak tower, pushing me in a carriage that only had three wheels. The fourth wheel had fallen off at some point, and spare parts were so hard to come by that she had not managed to get the wheel replaced. As she ran, a man was shot in front of her. His body immediately fell over the carriage, his blood dripping onto my coat. My mother had no time to cry, scream, or recoil in horror. She matter-of-factly pushed his body off me and kept running. In the chaos, Yvonne, who had been doing her best to keep up on her little three-year-old legs, accidentally got separated from us. Eventually, someone found her lost, scared, and in tears, and brought her to a school that had been converted into a shelter. There, Yvonne witnessed several gruesome displays that she would never forget, including a man whose intestines were hanging out of his stomach where he had been shot. She also saw a row of four soldiers, each of whom had had a leg blown off. They leaned against one another because they had no crutches to hold them up.

Meanwhile, my mother desperately put up signs and asked everyone she came across about her lost daughter. She was so overcome with grief over losing Yvonne that she considered killing me and herself to end the misery. After ten days of searching, my mother finally learned of Yvonne's whereabouts and raced over to the school. Upon her arrival, a woman pointed Yvonne to a window and happily cried out, "Look who is there!" There, my mother stood, blood and dirt smeared across her shirt, with me in the three-wheeled carriage by her side. For years afterward, Yvonne had nightmares about her experiences. I seem to have been traumatized as well; every time warplanes soared overhead, my hands would shake. My hands would remain unsteady throughout my childhood. Mama started to hold us even closer, wishing that her love could somehow overcome the damage the war had inflicted upon her little girls.

For another year, we endured many more bombings. The few city blocks that had remained intact did not stay that way for long, and many buildings that had already been damaged crumbled to the ground. Then on April 23, 1945, the Red Army surrounded Berlin. By then, the Wehrmacht had become so depleted that it was comprised mostly of some aging veterans of the First World War and boys who had been called up from Hitler Youth. Over the course of the next week, the Soviet offensive made steady progress in taking control of the city.

During one of the final bombings of the war, Russian soldiers entered the bunker where Mama,

Yvonne, and I had sought shelter. We trembled as the Russians looked over everyone in the room. We had heard horror stories of the brutality of the Soviet troops. One soldier stepped toward us and gestured for Yvonne. Even at the age of four, Yvonne was uncommonly pretty. Mama had made a practice of putting dirt on her face in hopes that if invading Russian troops should encounter her that they would leave her alone. My mother was initially terrified when he singled Yvonne out. But this Russian soldier spoke German and was gentle. He introduced himself as Vanya and sat down on a stool so that he was at Yvonne's height and appeared less intimidating and imposing. He then affectionately pulled her onto his lap. Perhaps he had a little girl of his own hundreds of miles away in St. Petersburg, Moscow, or Yekaterinburg. He gently stroked Yvonne's hair, told her that she was beautiful, and promised to return with a gift for her. He did indeed come back, presenting my sister with a small bundle containing an amber necklace and bracelet. She used the bundle as a pillow at night, but times had become so difficult that it was nearly impossible to keep anything of value. Someone stole the amber jewelry from under her head as we slept. Days later, my mother came across Vanya's body in the street. He was dead.

By the early hours of April 30, the Soviet troops were quickly approaching the Reich Chancellery. Hitler received word that the Zoo flak tower did not have enough ammunition to last another night. When the Soviet troops were within two blocks, Hitler shot himself in the head. On May 7, Germany officially surrendered to the Allied forces. I reached my second birthday a week later.

My beautiful mama with her black hair and blue eyes.

Grandmother with my mother and her only son, Nikolaus, who was killed at the front at the age of thirty-one years.

FROM RUBBLE TO CHAMPAGNE

My mother and her lover, Valentino. Glamour couple in their day in Berlin.

2

A CHILDHOOD AMONG THE RUBBLE

Year 1946–1956

In the years after the war ended, Berlin slowly staggered back to her feet. Her population had suffered greatly. Only 2.8 million of the city's original population of 4.3 million remained. The city's female population was especially vulnerable, and many of the invading Soviet troops took great liberties. Estimates of numbers of rape victims from Berlin's two main hospitals ranged from 95,000 to 130,000. The victims even included Jewish women who were returning from concentration camps. The statistics were horrific and tragic when it came to Berlin's Jewish population. Of the 160,000 Jews who had lived in Berlin before the rise of the Nazi Party, only about 8,000 survived. This included 4,700 Jews who were married to Aryans and were therefore not deported; 1,400 who had remained hidden in the city for the duration of the war; and 1,900 Jews who returned to Berlin from the death camps.

The infrastructure of the city seemed to mirror its traumatized people; Berlin lay in a state of utter ruin. Approximately six hundred thousand apartments had been destroyed, burned-out cars littered the streets, and monuments like the Brandenburg Gate, which the Nazis had used as a party symbol, were riddled with bullet holes. Approximately 80 percent of the city was destroyed. Historians have estimated that for every citizen of Berlin, there were about 1,060 cubic feet of rubble.

The earliest memories I have of the city are images of destruction. I vividly recall at four years old surveying the remains of an American airplane that had crashed into the roof of the *Kaufhaus des Westens* or KaDeWe, an iconic Berlin department store located close to my family's apartment. In the years before the war, the KaDeWe had been a symbol of wealth and prestige; a patron of the store could enjoy an afternoon in the tearoom, purchase tailored dresses, and then pick up caviar at the food court. But the partnership that owned the store was Jewish. Under the Nazis' race laws, the company was forced to sell it in 1933. During the course of the war, the Allied bombing damaged most of the store. After the American bomber crashed into it in 1943, it remained in a state of ruin. Eventually, its former Jewish owners returned and began the process of restoring it to its former glory.

Our apartment building on Wittenbergplatz miraculously survived the war, but the building to the left of it did not. But as it turned out, traces of the war remained in our apartment. One day, when I was about three or four, I was playing on the floor of the kitchen when I realized that a plank was loose. I lifted it and found three round objects. Unaware of what they were, I ran to Mama and announced that there were three fish in the floor. My mother went into the kitchen and realized that they were grenades. She immediately called the bomb squad and had them removed. As she watched them work, her heart beat quickly inside her chest. She had struggled to keep us alive during the war, only for us to come close to death once more.

Due to the extreme housing shortage, and because our apartment had been assigned to us by the government, we were forced to open our home to a couple, the Schumachers. Living with the Schumachers was often tumultuous. Herr Schumacher was a brutish and coarse man. He was not on speaking terms with his wife, a mousy woman who seemed to chirp when she spoke. Frau Schumacher did her best to avoid her husband, leaving the apartment early in the morning and returning only at night. She kept mostly to herself although she did once show me their room. A rope was tied across the middle of the room like a clothing line, dividing it into two sides. Her side was neat and orderly, but his side was dirty and messy. A large painting of a woman, who was not Frau Schumacher, hung over his bed. When I inquired about the identity of the woman, Frau Schumacher answered in her high-pitched little voice, "That's his whore."

Herr Schumacher's abusive behavior was not limited to his wife. One evening, he came across Mama in the kitchen where she was using an axe to chop up wooden boxes to light the stove. He picked a fight with her, which quickly turned physical, and my mother hit him with the blunt part of the axe. The commotion must have alerted the neighbors, who called in the police. I was sent down to the courtyard, where I paced in circles around the cobblestones, crying inconsolably, and praying over and over again, "God, please don't let them take Mama away." In the end, to my tremendous relief, my mother was not arrested. Shortly thereafter, the Schumachers moved out.

As a child, I had a different bond with my mother than any other child I knew. She loved her children fiercely and was determined to keep our family together no matter how difficult times became. When I was about five years old, a couple, who owned a restaurant on the bottom floor of our apartment building, offered to adopt me. Giving one or both of her children up would have freed her from feeding extra mouths and allowed her to return to the free-spirited existence she had led during the war. But my mother would not do it. Motherhood was her true calling, and she was a survivor who thrived in the most adverse of situations.

I returned her love with equal intensity. I clung to her constantly, at times obsessively, always seeking affection and reassurance. My sister was also very attached to her. Even as adults, we would talk about Mama with such heightened devotion that others would comment about our fixation with her. As children, she was the heart of our unit of three, and she did her best to fill the void our fathers had left. She regularly praised us and cuddled with us. She also preached to us about the right ways to behave and the importance of making good choices. On more than one occasion, she told us wistfully not to follow the example of how she lived her life.

Despite Mama's valiant love, however, I still struggled with a sense of worthlessness. Mama would tell me that I could accomplish anything I wanted and always saw the good in me. Her warm embrace was my only source of true happiness throughout my childhood. Nonetheless, the stigma of illegitimacy was too great for her love alone to overcome, especially when coupled with the many other challenges I faced. I tried to make up for what felt lacking in my life by trying to be as dutiful and helpful as possible. I strove to please others, to show them how good I could be, but Mama was the only person who seemed to notice my efforts.

Yvonne did not develop the same insecurities I did growing up. She continued to blossom as a beauty. Her dark hair, olive skin, and glowing brown eyes made her exotic when compared to most German children, who were typically fairer. By comparison, I was rather ordinary in appearance, with dirty blonde hair, bluish-gray eyes, and a round little head. Yvonne always presented herself in a refined manner. When praised enough, a child will learn to embody the subject of that praise. In Yvonne's case, she became aware of her good looks early on and took great pride in them. After a bath, Yvonne would appear just as clean and well-kept hours later, whereas I would become dirty again in about five minutes. On the street, strangers would remark how attractive she was while ignoring me even though I stood right by her side. I was very proud to have such a remarkable sister, but inside, it hurt that I never received the lavish praise and smiles that she did. Next to her, I felt like a street urchin.

When I was six years old, I began attending school. I was excited to go. I remember holding my notebook close to my chest, thinking to myself, "I am going to do really well in school. I am going to do my best." I was always eager for any opportunity to prove my worth and to better myself. But school provided me with a rude awakening. Whereas many of the other children had begun their educations in kindergarten, my sister and I had not started school until the first grade. This had not impacted Yvonne significantly. Even though she was an average student, she had no difficulty learning. But I struggled from the moment I stepped into the classroom. I could not follow the teacher and was unable to master concepts as well as my classmates. I know now that this was not because I was incapable of learning or due to any sort of learning disability but because I do not learn in conventional ways. I simply needed a different approach. But at the time, unfortunately, no pedagogical efforts had been developed to work with children like me, and my teacher was not creative or enlightened enough to see anything but a deviant child who was unable to embrace her methods. In home economics, where I learned to sew, the teacher became so frustrated with me that she slapped me across the face. At the end of the year, my teacher condemned me to my mother, stating, "She is dumb." I was required to repeat first grade. The blow was devastating to my already fragile ego. From then on, school felt like an assault on my self-esteem. To this day, I cannot stand schoolyards because they remind me of how I felt.

 The one positive experience I had at school was my friendship with Regina Berger, now Brade. She was unusually tall, which made us a funny pair because I was one of the shortest children in the class. We were often referred to as "the tall one and the short one." Like me, Regina did not have a father. He had fought in Africa during the war. Although he did survive, he disappeared instead of returning to his family. Perhaps he succumbed to a mental illness like so many shell-shocked soldiers or maybe he met another woman and chose to start a new life with her. Regina always did her homework neatly and, recognizing my difficulties in the classroom, generously allowed me to copy it. Regina was my only friend at school; I did not make friends easily. As an adult, although I have developed fine social skills over the years, I am still more of a loner, preferring solitude to spending time with others.

Throughout my childhood, my mother struggled to provide for our family. She had followed in her father's footsteps and worked as a hairdresser before the war. But after having children, she had stopped working, focusing her attention on taking care of us. After the war ended, she began to work in the black market, striking deals whenever she could. On one occasion, an entire wall of our apartment was filled with cans of grapefruit juice that had been imported from the United States. Another time, we came home to find a motorcycle in the middle of our fourth-floor apartment. She also brought in some earnings sewing brassieres. She also saved money wherever possible. Instead of taking our shoes to a cobbler, she put the soles on our shoes herself. The result was crude-looking but good enough to keep shoes on our feet.

But my mother's income was not sufficient to feed us well. Hunger was a constant companion throughout my childhood. My greatest dream was to eat enough to know what it was like to be full. Each day at lunchtime at school, Regina would unwrap two pieces of black bread and several slices of thick uncooked bacon, which she claimed she hated. She always gave the bacon to me, which I relished. It felt like a luxury compared to what I ate outside at home. After school or on weekends, I would go to an open-air market that was held on a large plaza close to the apartment. I would gather the discarded wooden boxes that had been used to transport fish. Mama would chop them up to feed the fire in the stove so that she could cook. After the KaDeWe reopened in 1950, it became a source of bounty for me. I went into the glamorous store armed with a small metal pail and would take fish or chicken heads or any entrails that were otherwise going to be thrown away. My mother would use them to make soups. On occasion, I was able to procure orange crates, and sometimes, there I would find half of an orange that was past ripe. I took anything that was edible, knowing that Mama would figure out how to make do with it. The KaDeWe employees were eager to see their institution's former glory restored and were not pleased to see a waif of a girl asking for scraps. They looked upon me with disdain. I started telling them that I was collecting scraps for my cat, hoping to bring some dignity into the situation. But on one occasion, the man working behind the counter cruelly inquired, "Are you really asking for the cat?" Humiliated, I wished in that moment that I could sink into the floor. But his comment did not deter me from my mission. I was too hungry.

FROM RUBBLE TO CHAMPAGNE

Despite these hardships, I still found ways to play and have fun. Although my mother repeatedly admonished me not to go into the ruins, Regina and I often went anyway, looking for treasure. The ruins had already been picked over many times, and we never found anything, but the possibility was still exciting to us. Sometimes we would follow an organ grinder around, waiting for passersby to throw down a few coins. We delighted in helping him to collect his earnings. Other times, we made do with objects we could find at home. A wooden crate with a string tied to it became the perfect wagon for a doll. Or on the rare occasion that Mama was able to procure a wheel of Camembert cheese, we kept the box it came in, repurposing it as storage for our most cherished objects. Occasionally, we played in the courtyard behind the apartment building. We would drape a tarp and play house or simulate a grocery store using stones for potatoes. We often became too animated and rowdy in our play, causing our neighbors, who were not tolerant of excessively noisy children, to chase us away. When relegated to the street, we would draw circles on the asphalt and play hopscotch. My favorite playtime activity was marbles. I yearned for glass marbles, but Mama was never willing to spend her hard-earned money on something so trivial, so I started out with clay marbles. Several of my playmates, however, brought their glass marbles to our games. The winner got to keep a glass marble. Overtime, with much practice and determination, I was able to accumulate several glass marbles. I would hold them in my hand and run my hand over the smooth surface relishing my victories. It was the closest I had ever felt to being wealthy.

In 1951, when I was seven and a half years old and Yvonne was ten, Mama announced that a man was coming into our lives. My mother had first met Georg Schneider when they were schoolmates as children. Georg was a tailor who came from a long line of tailors. Indeed, his name, Schneider, means tailor. Mama and Georg had reconnected after he returned to Berlin from a Siberian prison camp. Of the eighteen million men who had served in the Wehrmacht, only one-third survived. Although Georg was among the fortunate few who made it through the war, the five years he spent incarcerated were horrific. The prisoners were forced into backbreaking work, such as building roads and digging out mines, all at freezing temperatures. The Russians put him to work mending uniforms, which was physically less taxing than hard labor and allowed him to stay indoors away from the cold. But Georg still suffered from malnourishment. The prisoners constantly lived on the brink of starvation; in any given winter, as much as 25 percent of the prison population died from hunger. In his desperation, Georg once stole a piece of bread, which was a major crime. He received a severe beating as punishment.

Mama announced that Yvonne and I now had a father. Delighted, I called him Papa right away, but Yvonne was more hesitant. At first,

I relished having a father. He was industrious and found a job in custom tailoring for a local business. I started assisting him by delivering suits to his customers. Among his clients was famed German actor O. E. Hasse, who would later appear in the 1953 Alfred Hitchcock film *I Confess* with Montgomery Clift and Anne Baxter, as well as the 1954 film *Betrayed* with Clark Gable and Lana Turner. When I delivered his order to him, Hasse took a moment to give me an affectionate pat on my head. Due to his hard work, Georg was able to provide for us. For the first time, we could eat regular meals, and Mama no longer had to work on the black market. He also made clothing for us, which felt luxurious compared to the ordinary clothes I was used to wearing. Mama became his muse, and he created beautiful suits for her that emphasized her tiny waist and trim figure. She looked like a glamorous movie star.

But the euphoria ended soon after Georg moved into our apartment. We began to see another side of him. Although he continued to work hard during the week, he started to spend his weekends drinking. He did not exhibit the violent or sloppy behavior of some drunkards but instead became quiet. Sometimes he just disappeared. On what was supposed to be our first Christmas Eve together, we waited for hours for him to come home, but he never showed up. He and Mama fought constantly, abusing each other verbally. At times, in her anger, Mama even threw plates at the ground. On one occasion, my mother tore a shelf off the wall and hit him with it, breaking it to pieces. Georg also seemed unable to cope with happiness or good humor. Whenever we laughed or displayed some form of levity, he would get into a bad mood and deflate our spirits. I wonder now if his years in Siberia were so traumatic that he no longer knew how to be joyful.

Yvonne and I could see how miserable Mama was and begged her to leave him. But our pleas were to no avail. There were so few men in

Germany at that time, and Georg was her best option for a meal ticket. It was simply too difficult trying to survive with two children only on a meager income from the government. Yvonne and I had no choice but to accept that he was now a permanent part of our lives. As I watched them fight, I vowed to myself that when I got married, I would only choose someone with whom I could have a harmonious relationship.

Despite Georg's contributions to our family, we still struggled financially. Mama turned to the church for assistance. Although she was not a devout Catholic in any way, when I was ten, Mama decided to have Yvonne and me baptized so that we could use the church as a resource. My name following my confirmation became Vivianne Maria Isabella.

Although Georg provided us with enough that we were no longer hungry, Yvonne and I were still malnourished and underweight. Mama soon learned of a program through which the church sent children away to gain weight for their health. We spent the summer of 1953 in a camp in the Black Forest in the southwest of Germany. The camp was well-organized and rigorous. Our routine included waking up at six o'clock every morning, engaging in calisthenics, picking blueberries in the forest, taking naps, and eating nutritious meals. This new exposure to the outdoors did have some drawbacks, however. Yvonne and I both had lice, which meant that our chaperones had to powder our heads to get rid of them. Yvonne, who treasured her luxurious black locks, cried as they put the powder into her tresses. But to me, the powder was a small price to pay for the natural wonders around us. Although Berlin was springing back to life after the ravages of war, rubble still constituted the majority of our landscape, and we only saw a few sparse patches of grass there. By contrast, the verdant meadows and dark green woods of the Black Forest were utterly enchanting to me. For the first time, I began to appreciate the beauty of nature and realized how it fed my soul just as the food I received replenished my body. I began to dream of one day having a house with a garden. I could have stayed in the paradise of the camp forever, but I missed Mama so much that my heart hurt. At the end of the six weeks, Yvonne and I, now both at a healthy weight, returned to our mother's loving arms.

Aside from our sojourn in the Black Forest, we did occasionally leave Berlin to visit our relatives. Our maternal grandmother, whom we called Oma, resided outside Berlin in a suburb called Wittenau. Although it now has skyscrapers, at the time, Wittenau had the feel of a sleepy country village. A few times a year, we would take the bus out to Wittenau to visit her. Oma lived with her youngest daughter, Eva, who was thirteen years younger than Mama. Eva was Oma's favorite daughter, and by default, her daughter Michele was Oma's preferred grandchild. This meant that Oma always gave Michele the biggest apple or an egg if she was able to procure one. Perhaps Oma felt a special kinship with Eva because she too lost a son; Eva's little boy had succumbed to diphtheria when he was three years old. I was not jealous of Michele for having the majority of Oma's affection. I simply accepted that I was not close to her.

Mama's other sister Theodora Pöllmann was a year younger than her. Theodora was married to an engineer named Roland. They had a daughter, Margot, who was a year older than I was, and a son, Georg, whom we called Schorschi. I was born in between my two cousins; Datschi was a year older than me, and Schorschi was a year younger. After the end of the war, Berlin had been divided into East Berlin—the Soviet sector—and West Berlin, which combined the sectors that the United States, United Kingdom, and France controlled. Whereas Mama's apartment fell in West Berlin, the Pöllmanns's home lay in East Berlin.

Visiting my cousins was a window into a different world. As time went on, West Berlin experienced a resurgence. Industries developed, businesses grew, and new stores opened. West Berliners began to enjoy fashion, consumer goods, automobiles, and an increasingly comfortable lifestyle. But the moment we approached the border to East Berlin, we could sense a dramatic difference. To cross the border, we had to undergo intense questioning. In the Pöllmann house, we could no longer listen to the radio stations we enjoyed just a few miles away in our apartment. Neighbors reported on one another for any action or activity that could be construed as insurgency against Communist ideology. Western films and books were banned, and even hitchhiking was condemned as Westernized degenerate behavior. The KaDeWe, which had returned to the echelon of luxury it had known before the war, was construed in East Berlin as a horrific monument to indulgence and decadence. Turning their backs on Western ways, East Berliners wore bland and cheaply made clothes that were produced in state-owned companies. The coins in East German currency were made from aluminum and did not have the substantive weight of money from the West. Purchasing a car entailed waiting between ten and twelve years, and even after the long wait, one could only obtain a vehicle through a connection to a member of the Socialist Party. Notably, the Party members did live better than the rest of the population. They enjoyed privileges, such as regular access to fresh oranges and real coffee and resided in comfortable large homes. Several of them lived in the same neighborhood as my cousins and we could observe their extravagant lifestyles firsthand. During every visit, I thought about how I would die if I had grown up in such an environment, unable to express myself or to think my own thoughts without fear of reprisals. But ironically, between their intact family and my uncle Roland's job as an engineer, the Pöllmanns lived better in East Berlin than Mama, Yvonne, and I did in the West.

As Yvonne and I grew older, we continued to maintain a close relationship. Mama raised us to get along well and to care for each other. Although we occasionally fought like all sisters do, for the most part, we enjoyed our special bond. Yvonne kept up her good looks in her teenage years and grew into a proud, lovable, charming, and outgoing young woman. I continued to take great pride in having such a beautiful sister.

When I was eleven, I started keeping a "Poesie Album," or friendship book, a popular pastime among preteens and teenagers in Germany. Girls kept drawings, photographs, pictures, notes, and other sentimental items in the pages of their Poesie Albums and asked friends and family members to contribute to it. My mother wrote the following poem for me, which rhymed in the original German.

> Viva, do not forget when you
> find happiness in life.
> Do not forget that there is still
> your sister, Yvonne.

> Do not fight and always love
> one another,
> And I will find my peace.

I sometimes wondered why Mama asked me to take care of Yvonne. After all, my sister had the advantage of her good looks and had a more positive outlook on life than I did. Some people might have said that Yvonne was her pride and joy or even her favorite. But Mama was so devoted to me that I always felt secure in her love. Perhaps she just wanted to ensure that Yvonne and I would always support each other regardless of the uncertainty in our lives at home and in the world around us.

A year later, when I turned twelve, my mother was required to apply for a residence permit for me. My mother found the process infuriating. She tried to explain to the bureaucrats in charge that I had never even seen a country aside from Germany, but they insisted on enforcing the rules. In Germany, children were given the nationality of their fathers. Because her father was not a German citizen, Mama was considered a Yugoslavian national even though she had been born and raised in Germany and did not speak Serbian. In my case, due to my illegitimacy, I was considered stateless in the eyes of the German government and was listed as such on my mother's passport. The experience was utterly deflating for me and amplified the feelings of worthlessness that had persisted throughout my childhood. As much as my mother tried to pass off the situation as bureaucratic nonsense, I could not help but absorb its humiliating implication. I felt that I was born lesser than other children through no fault of my own, denied recognition while Germany was proud to proclaim so many others as hers. As hard as you may try to fight it, the perceptions of others does make your reality.

But on the other side of the despair, I so often felt was an all-consuming desire to improve my station in life. All around me, I saw people who were so weary from the war and the hard times that followed that they simply accepted whatever life put in their paths. I, however, grew up yearning for acceptance, reassurance, respect, and dignity. This sense of wanting more for myself must have been innate. I felt it as far back as I can remember. I saw myself as a seeker; I constantly sought opportunities to better myself. I often observed my mother's friend Charlotte and pondered how I could emulate her. I admired her beauty and how she always comported herself in an elegant and refined manner. She dressed well, spoke intelligently, and was happily married to an antique dealer. They lived in a comfortable apartment, enjoyed delicious meals, and were treated with approval and high regard in German society. My highest aspiration was to grow up to have a life like hers.

In 1956, a new opportunity came to my family and me. One of our neighbors had a relative in Edmonton, Canada, and they started talking about moving there themselves. My mother was immediately intrigued. Mama had always had a yearning to leave Germany. She had been to Prague once, but aside from that, she had never visited another country. But she had maintained an interest her entire life to travel and see other parts of the globe. Everyone she spoke with had a highly romanticized notion of Canada, calling it the Land of Milk and Honey. My mother came away with the impression that we could have a much better life there. Georg was hesitant at first, but my mother was relentless in her efforts to convince him.

Georg and Mama decided to get married to make immigration easier, but he did not adopt Yvonne or me. He probably would have been open to adoption and making us his daughters officially, but Mama did not want him to have any authority over us. She explained that she was only marrying him out of convenience. Neither of us were offended. Although we appreciated how hard he worked to provide for us, we had witnessed too many fights and instances of drunken behavior to feel disappointment. Instead, we focused our attention on our excitement over immigrating. Georg went to Canada first in order to establish himself there and planned to send for us later. Whenever a letter from him arrived in the mail, we huddled around it and parsed every word, eager for any details of what our future home was like.

Finally, in December of that year, when I was thirteen years old and Yvonne was fifteen, our tickets arrived. We traveled from Berlin to Hamburg, where we boarded the ship that would take us across the Atlantic Ocean. Despite of all the negative experiences I had had in Germany, I still cried as the ship made its way into the water. I was leaving behind all that I had ever known. But then an image came into my mind. I visualized myself returning to Berlin one day. I imagined an older version of myself, refined and beautiful, wearing a suit that was far more expensive and luxurious than the ones Georg made for Mama. I would be able to dine in Berlin's finest restaurants and stay in the city's most exclusive hotels. Those who had looked down upon me would not even recognize me. I envisioned myself as the person I had always wanted to be. I wiped my tears away and looked back at my homeland until I could no longer see the shore. Then I turned the other way, toward my future.

My sister and I as little children.

Myself at the age of six. The time when I began to search for food and wooden boxes for the fire.

3

IN THE LAND OF MILK AND HONEY

Year 1956–1960

It took us twelve days to sail the 3,200 miles from Hamburg, Germany, to Halifax, Nova Scotia. The journey was a difficult one. Traveling in December meant encountering high winds and cold weather. The crew tied down tables and chairs for fear that a violent gust would drive them into a passenger or overboard. In order to move about the deck, we walked along ropes. Many of the passengers became seasick, and early into our voyage, the ship already reeked of vomit. By the time we arrived in Halifax, we were beyond grateful to stand on dry land. But we did not remain in Halifax for long. Instead, we boarded a train and traveled almost eight hundred miles more to Montreal.

Georg met us at the train station and brought us to our new home. He had rented an apartment in a building that looked like barracks. These austere, cheaply built eyesores were and still are characteristic of immigrant housing in many cities across Europe and North America. But the ugliness of the exterior did not faze us, especially after we saw the interior of our new apartment. For the first time, we had central heating and a bathtub, which made it feel like we had stepped into a world of utter grandeur. Yvonne and I also had a proper bedroom, which we had not had in Berlin. Georg had found functional, comfortable furniture for the apartment, which he paid off overtime. As a crowning glory, there was a tray on the kitchen table filled with bananas, pineapples, and chocolates. For the girl who had begged for scraps, it was a sight to behold.

But the idyllic veneer of our new lives quickly gave way to a harsher reality. Georg's drinking had tapered off significantly before he left Germany and had ceased altogether once he moved to Canada. The verbal assaults he and Mama inflicted upon each other, however, were just as brutal as they had always been. Our new and beautiful apartment soon came to know their barbs and vitriol. Upon arriving in Montreal, Georg had immediately set out to find work, but he was unable to obtain a job as a tailor. Instead, he was only able to find menial jobs that only immigrants and Canadians down on their luck were willing to take. On one occasion, he was hired to tar a roof. During the course of the construction, a pail fell on to his head. Georg was rushed to the hospital where the staff shaved the back of his head to conduct their examination. He luckily was not seriously harmed and returned home with a large bump but no further injuries. Georg continued to look for other jobs, but once again, we descended to the same desperation we had experienced back in Germany. We spent our first winter in Canada hungry.

Mama only knew of one place to ask for help. She went to the church and brought me along. Yvonne refused to come along. She was too proud. I too was embarrassed about having to beg, but I was willing to do what it took to help my family survive. With what little English we knew, my mother and I attempted to explain our plight to the priest. He listened sympathetically and handed us $35. My mother immediately used it to purchase flour, rice, and other items that would last for a long time and could get us through the next few weeks.

I began to attend school upon my arrival in Montreal. I had learned a little English in Germany and managed to pick it up quickly in Canada. But school in Montreal proved just as tortuous as it had in Berlin. I could not follow the teachers or keep up with my classmates there either. I sat at my desk each day staring at the clock, willing time to go faster.

I most looked forward to the time after school when I could go to my neighbor's apartment. She was also a German immigrant. She made a decent income cleaning houses and had the ultimate luxury: a black-and-white television. I had never had regular access to a television set before and thought that it was marvelous. My favorite program was *I Love Lucy*. Watching Lucy, Ricky, Fred, and Ethel's hilarious antics was a welcome reprieve from the challenges of school and settling into Montreal. Learning to understand and appreciate humor is always one of the greatest challenges in mastering a new language, and Lucy proved a wonderful teacher. Soon I started making sense of colloquialisms, puns, jokes, and punch lines.

One afternoon, instead of rushing off to watch television, I found myself in front of a mirror, staring intensely at my face in the reflection. As a child, I had constantly asked questions, eager to comprehend my life and the world around me, but I found no answers. But that day was different from any day I had ever had before. My concentration grew stronger as I focused in on my reflection. "Who am I?" I asked. "Who are you? Who is Viva?" What happened next defies standard logic. Normally, we interact with the world by processing information that comes through our five senses. We ground our thoughts in the data that our senses feed us about our environment and circumstances. As I gazed at myself, I initially noticed the thoughts in my mind, the sensations in my body, and the surroundings around me. I asked the questions again and again and focused in on my face. My thoughts started to disappear, and my awareness of my body and my physical location diminished until I lost all conception of mind and body. All that remained was an intense stillness. And then suddenly, I returned back to my regular state of consciousness.

I know now that I had gone into deep meditation. As you move into that state, you first loosen the constraints of self-centeredness and ego. "Who am I?" becomes "I am" and then "I" and then dissipates. You enter a realm of non-sensory information where you do not need to compute or rationalize the way that you do in the every day. There is a connection to the energy or life force of the universe. Boundaries fall away, and there is a sense of utter unity.

To many people, deep meditation is beautiful, peaceful, and nourishing to the soul. But at the tender age of fourteen and coming from an environment when nobody was even aware of meditation, I had no idea what had happened to me. I was terrified. I wondered what was wrong with me or if I was broken or damaged in some way. There was no one with whom I could discuss it. For my entire life, I had desperately craved acceptance and approval, and I was convinced that if anyone knew about my experience, I would be condemned as crazy. Even my loving mother would not have understood. I tried to banish the episode to the back recesses of my mind and said nothing about it to anyone for over four decades.

After we had been in Canada for a year, my family was still struggling financially. Georg did his best to find opportunities to earn money, but there was not always work to be found. My family could not depend on Georg's inconsistent earnings alone. Our neighbor introduced my mother to wealthy families who needed housekeeping. Yvonne got a job at a cigarette filter factory. Under Canadian child labor laws, I, at fourteen and a half, was too young to work. But Mama successfully obtained a special permit from the government, allowing me to seek employment, so I was able to leave school to get a job.

I had no qualms about ending my formal education. I had never enjoyed school, and I thought that I could better myself more as a working woman. I looked older than my age because I was fully developed and curvy. I had a peaches and cream complexion, and after years in my beautiful sister's shadow, I had become attractive in my own right. I could also speak English fluently and felt ready to enter the working world. I had always had a great capacity to work, and I was eager to do it.

My first job was full of promise. I joined the office of a Polish dentist who wanted to train me to become a dental assistant. I worked daily from nine o'clock in the morning to nine o'clock at night for $15 a week. I knew from the beginning that I was paid too little for the hours I put in and that my boss was stingy with money. But I did not complain but instead keeping the long-term benefits of building a career in mind. Overtime, the hours became more regular, and I started working from nine in the morning until five in the afternoon. In the morning, I was tasked with cleaning the office. It was particularly challenging trying to keep the louver blinds clean, which collected dust easily. I also scrubbed the floors and counters of the office. At noon, I would change into a white uniform with a nurse's hat. I appreciated the opportunity to look professional. No one would have guessed that I was fourteen. Among my duties was to answer the phone, which I did in a friendly but responsible voice, mixing the plaster for the molds, developing X-rays, and sterilizing instruments. If I had fulfilled my duties for the day and my boss had some downtime, he would ask me to trim his fingernails. I did not mind since I was always happier when I was busy.

One day, as I was sitting at my desk in my white uniform, the doctor's friend, a man in his forties, came in to see him. I had met his friend before because he came in from time to time. But instead of passing by me with a quick hello, this time, he grabbed me and put his hands all over my body. I backed away and gently pushed him out the door, still trying to be friendly. Sexual harassment was not something that was discussed in those days, and many women felt that they had to tolerate it to keep their jobs. After he left, I felt embarrassed and ashamed. I was afraid to tell my boss about the encounter and felt uneasy talking about it. The notion of describing where and how he touched me was mortifying. I was also worried that I would lose my job for what had happened. I vacillated for some time on whether to say anything, weighing the options in my mind and examining both scenarios. Ultimately, I decided to tell him because I was worried that his friend would come back and repeat the behavior. Fortunately, my boss believed me, which was not always the case among women who reported these experiences. My boss became irate and assured me that he would reprimand his friend and not allow him to come back to the office. I never saw the friend again.

Despite my boss's defense of me, I felt that he took advantage of my youth and inexperience by making me work hard but never offering me a raise. I was not learning as much as I had hoped and saw no future in the job. After a year, I decided that it was time for me to move on and find another job.

My next job was at Woolworths, a five-and-dime store. I worked behind the lunch counter, making sandwiches and salads. I truly enjoyed the work there. I have always been domestic and love to cook. Even though I was only preparing food and not cooking at Woolworths, I took great pride in my work. I always gave my customers a generous amount of toppings and made each item with care and heart. Pleasing people and being of service were qualities that had been with me since I was a child, and I was delighted to give my customers a good experience.

In addition to bringing home my earnings, I tried to save wherever possible to help my family. Instead of paying $0.15 for bus fare, I walked to work even on Montreal's harshest winter days. I obtained my clothes secondhand from a wealthy woman whose house Mama cleaned. She was about my size, and even her old shoes fit me. Her knit dresses were all high quality, and she charged my mother two or three dollars for each one. She could have easily afforded to give the clothes to us, but she was not willing to let us have them for free. I would have preferred to wear something more youthful than her clothes, such as the big sweaters that were in style for girls my age, but I was grateful for what Mama was able to procure.

Shortly after I started working at Woolworths, a trio of medical students from McGill University started coming to the lunch counter. One of them was Peter, a twenty-year-old French Canadian. He was tall and handsome with dark hair and a serious countenance. I appreciated how mature and dependable he appeared to be; I was always interested in older men and looked for someone who had the qualities of a father figure. Peter invited me to go out with him. We started going to the movies together, where we would hold hands and kiss. The son of a judge, Peter was smart, well-mannered, and respectful, and he never tried to pressure me to do anything with which I was uncomfortable. He had character and had received a good upbringing.

As much as I liked Peter, I purposefully did not tell my mother about him. I was not worried that she would dislike him—indeed, I believe that she would have approved of him and seen him as a good match for me. But I was concerned about Peter meeting Georg. By this point, Georg had managed to find a job as a tailor, which did lift his spirits and enable him to better provide, but these improvements were not enough to outweigh his negative qualities. He had started to make irrational and incorrect presumptions about my sister and her romantic life. When she dated someone, he accused her of comporting herself in a permissive or even promiscuous manner. But in reality, she did not engage in these behaviors. Worried that if Georg learned about my boyfriend, he would turn his suspicions and imputations to me, I kept silent about Peter's presence in my life.

Although I was no longer in school and working, I was still determined to find ways to educate and better myself. I felt a strong yearning toward self-improvement, vowing that each day, I would be further along on my journey than the day before. I have never relied upon luck. Instead, I believe that you must use whatever tools or opportunities are at your disposal to plan out your life. Despite my negative experiences in school, I was always eager to learn. My passion to learn is still strong to this day. As a teenager, I became a member of the *Bertelsmann Lesering*, a German language reading circle organized by the Bertelsmann Publishing House. I was able to order books through a subscription and receive discounted prices. I wanted to make sure to maintain my German and to develop reading skills in my native language. Many of the books that arrived were romance novels.

During this time, I also started to attend night school in order to learn typing and stenography, which I hoped would help me to develop the requisite skills for an office job. One day, after I had been at Woolworths for six months, I had just finished cleaning for the day when the manager asked me to clean off the underside of the counter. When I bent down to begin the task, I discovered numerous wads of chewing gum that customers had stuck under the counter. As I scraped off each piece of gum, I felt deeply humiliated. I felt in that moment that I was being lowered below my worth. Something inside me told me that I needed to make a change.

Soon after I turned sixteen, I looked in the local newspaper for job listings. I decided to apply for a position in the sales and services office of a Volkswagen (VW) dealership. Peter, who happened to own a Bug, VW's most iconic car, drove me to the interview during my lunch break. He patiently waited downstairs as I convinced some executives of my qualifications. An hour later, I emerged with a new job in the accounting department.

Frau Meier, a German woman, headed the department. She was friendly and kind and immediately took me under her wing. She was also in charge of doling out my assignments. I did everything I was instructed in a timely fashion and always with a smile. This included making coffee for the entire department and running errands at the bank. I rarely had enough tasks to fill my day and felt that I did not earn the money I was paid. I was unable to take pride in my work, which I found deflating.

The office environment and staff were equally uninspiring. We worked in a large sterile room that was filled with desks. Most of the staff were women in their forties, more than twice my age. They seemed like mindless drones, running numbers, stamping documents, and filing papers. I could not relate to them and did not feel a sense of comradery. There was no passion, no energy, and no commitment to growth in that room. Instead, the atmosphere was stale and stifling.

A few months after I started working at VW, I called Peter and told him that I did not want to see him any longer. As much as I respected and liked Peter, I did not feel that there was enough of a spark between us to continue. A few days later, Peter called and said that he had been so distraught over the breakup that, in keeping with his faith, he had consulted with a Catholic priest. But I had no interest in reconciling with him. Looking back, I now regret that I ended the relationship in such an insensitive manner. Although I was generally thoughtful and compassionate at that age, I now see that I was not generous in sharing those qualities with him. From his perspective, it must have been quite heartbreaking. But youth is all about making mistakes and learning from them. I never saw him again after that.

By this point in time, I had grown past some of the feelings of worthlessness that had accompanied me throughout my childhood. They were like a wound from the past that had healed to leave behind a faint scar. The memory was still there, but my drive to improve myself and work ethic had reduced those feelings to a dormant state. But in their place, a new demon began to loom over me. I started to feel incredibly unhappy. I began each day at VW with dread. As I climbed the staircase that led to my floor, I would dig my fingers into the railing as a voice inside my head repeated, "I hate this! I hate this!" I felt an all-consuming emptiness as I shuffled through the few responsibilities Frau Meier assigned to me. Looking around at my coworkers, I felt stuck. I did not want their lives to be my future; the idea of spending decades in such a stagnant environment felt miserable. But the longer I stayed there, the harder it was to imagine any other option. It felt as if all my efforts to better myself had failed. I had spiraled into a deep, dark well of depression, and I did not see how I could get myself out of it.

Toward the end of my time at Woolworths, I had saved enough money to purchase a used VW Karmann Ghia. I kept it in a garage I had rented in a duplex that neighbored the building where I lived. One day, I felt that I could not stand the misery any longer. I did the unthinkable: I decided that I was going to take my life. I went into the garage, closed the door, and started the motor. I had heard somewhere that the carbon monoxide would render you unconscious, and soon, I could end my pain. As I waited to drift off to my ultimate end, a little girl of about six years old appeared in front of me. She had chin-length hair and wore a short dress. She was probably the daughter of the owner of the duplex.

"What are you doing?" she asked.

I glanced over and realized that I had forgotten that there was a side door that led into the garage, which is how she must have come in. I immediately snapped to attention, opened the garage door, and turned off the motor.

"I am getting ready to wash my car," I answered meekly.

She accepted my answer and skipped off, blissfully unaware that she had just saved my life.

I have often thought about that little girl over the years. I don't even know her name. Was there a greater force at work on that day that sent her to rescue me? Are we predestined to enter the world on a specific date and to leave it on another? These are questions to which there is currently no answer. All I know is that she drew me back from the chasm of death and changed my course from dying to living.

It is one of the trappings of youth that there is little sense of perspective. After my own experience, I see how easy it is for young people to succumb to their inner turmoil and become depressed and suicidal. There is no awareness that circumstances can change and that things can get better with time. Life is not static; it will change even if you are happy and do not want it to. It is one of the blessings of getting older that you can leave the chaos and struggles of youth behind. There is also a self-centeredness that often inflicts the young. I realize now that I had never even considered at that moment what my death would do to my mother. Now with the benefit of the passage of time, I am able to observe young people who are struggling without judging or imposing moral values on them. This is another gift of aging. I understand that their pain is real to them and that their hopelessness feels true inside their minds and hearts. Any young person who hurts the way that I did deserves compassion, love, support, and acceptance.

Today, there is a great stigma about depression and mental health. This was even more the case when I was seventeen. I had nowhere to turn and no one in whom I could confide about my suicide attempt. My family would have deemed me crazy, and Mama probably would have slapped me and told me to move on. But in my life, I have been very fortunate to receive the blessing of helping hands in the guise of ordinary people. Just as the little girl had appeared at just the right moment, I received assistance when I needed it the most from my cousin Datschi.

The Pöllmanns had immigrated to Canada two years after my family in 1958, as had my mother's other sister, Eva, and her family. Our grandmother followed in 1959. Datschi and I soon became best friends. She was a sensitive person who said that people did not always understand her. Perhaps as two individuals who did not always feel comprehended by the people around us, we became closer. Datschi played a pivotal role in my recovery process. I did not tell her about my suicide attempt or that I was depressed, but maybe she somehow knew how much I was hurting on a subconscious or energetic level. She and her brother, Schorschi, both had an incredible sense of humor. They were so funny that on numerous occasions, they made me laugh so hard that tears came to my eyes despite the tumult I was feeling. I was not someone who knew how to induce humor in others, but I appreciated it immensely. The laughter Datschi and Schorschi brought me was like medicine. It revitalized my spirit. The late American poet and memoirist Maya Angelou once wrote, "I've learned that people will forget what you said, people will forget what you did, but people will never forget how you made them feel." Datschi made me feel that it was possible to be happy once more, and I am forever grateful to her for that.

I picked myself up and went back to my daily routine. Work in the accounting department continued. On occasion, a senior executive came up to the accounting floor to speak with Frau Meier. He was in his forties, confident, and handsome. Whenever he was in close proximity, I felt an energy coming off him. Maybe it was pheromones. All I knew was that I liked it. It was an experience I had never had before. I had felt such a magnetic pull toward him, which I had never had with Peter. I knew that an attraction was developing between us, but I realized that it could go nowhere because he was married. One evening, after a Christmas party, he insisted on driving me home. I could tell from the way he helped me into my coat that my feelings were requited. He invited me for dinner, but I did not accept. Nothing ever transpired between us, not even a kiss.

As my work in the accounting department continued, I set my sights on a new goal. I had always wanted to be around people and in the center of activity. The service department, which was on the ground floor of the dealership, seemed like it would afford a much more robust experience than the accounting department. Given how much I had enjoyed waiting on customers at Woolworths and how service-oriented I was, the possibility of working directly with customers appeared a much better fit for my interests and abilities. Finally, a position became available as a secretary for the service manager. I would get to sit right outside the service manager's office and interact with every customer who came in. I immediately leaped at the opportunity and got the job.

But once again, the position was far from ideal. The service manager was an unattractive man with a horrible laugh. He also had a penchant for inappropriate behavior and tried to seduce me repeatedly. Although he did not put his hands on me, he would speak to me in an inappropriate manner. On one occasion, when my car was in the shop for service, he gave me a lift home. His foot drifted over to my side and got so close that it almost rubbed against mine. He also tried to convince me to come into his house to see it while his wife was away in Germany, which I refused. Another colleague from the service department, who claimed that he had royal blood, was even more brazen. After giving me a ride home one evening, he forced himself on to me and kissed me right on the mouth. I slapped his face as hard as I could, to which he just laughed. Sexual harassment was common in those days, and few people questioned it. Most women had no recourse but to accept it as normal behavior and just live with it.

In addition to my job at the service department on Mondays through Fridays, I also worked two other jobs on weekends. On Saturday mornings, I worked as a switchboard operator for VW Sales and Services. Then, in the afternoon, I would go to Woolworths and work the afternoon shift. I also put in a full day at Woolworths on Sundays. Datschi continued to keep my spirits up. On numerous Saturday mornings, I would pick up calls at the switchboard, answering, "Volkswagen Sales and Services." Datschi would be on the other line, and she would say, just one word, "Fiat." I would laugh, and she would immediately brighten my day with her prank.

From time to time, I would have a weekend off. Datschi, Schorschi, Yvonne, and I would go to Mount Royale, a small mountain west of downtown Montreal. We would enjoy ice-skating and spend fifteen cents for the entire day, which meant getting french fries and a coffee. When I was about seventeen and a half and was able to take more time off, Datschi and I took a bus all the way to Miami. We stayed in a cheap hotel, danced, met other people our age, and had good fun. I had also gone to Miami before with my parents and sister when I was fifteen. Datschi and I marveled over the palm trees and the ocean, which felt so foreign and novel to a pair of German-born teenagers living in Canada. Laughing with Datschi in the Florida sunshine, I had finally found my way back to happiness.

4

LOVE

Year 1961–1964

On November 4, 1961, when I was eighteen and Yvonne was twenty, my sister got married. Her husband, Erik Andersen, was an immigrant from Denmark. He was a handsome man with a warm personality and a zest for life. He was a wonderful match for my beautiful and charming sister. I immediately took to him and saw him as the brother I had never had. Like us, Erik had known what it was like to struggle to make ends meet. He worked as a painter and also pursued interior design. When I turned nineteen, I moved into

Yvonne and Erik's home. I was eager to live on my own, but Mama would not let me. She had decided that she did not want me to live alone until I was twenty-one. Moving to my sister's house, however, was an acceptable compromise. I loved living there. Yvonne was orderly, clean, and had a good sense of how to make her home cheerful and attractive. Even something as simple as sitting around her living room swapping stories over cups of coffee was a true pleasure.

Having seen my sister fall in love and get married, I was eager to find someone with whom to share my life. But after my experience with Peter, I knew that I needed someone with whom I felt a powerful and meaningful connection. I had several ideas in mind for my potential match. I was looking for a father figure and someone who was stable and had potential. Good looks alone would not suffice. I wanted a person of substance who shared in my ambition to get ahead.

In 1963, shortly after I turned twenty, a young German man came into VW to purchase a car. He was tall, slender, and handsome with clear blue eyes. He had a clean-cut appearance, and he wore his ash-blond hair neatly combed to one side. His warm smile revealed a set of perfect white teeth. He offered me a friendly wink, to which I responded with a pleasant grin, but I was not intrigued and forgot about him the moment he left.

A few days later, the adjuster from the service department came over to my desk and stated that the German man who had recently come in had been asking about me. The adjuster then informed me that the car the man had purchased was a brand-new Porsche. Although I would never choose a man based on the type of car he drove, the fact that a young immigrant could afford a new Porsche suggested that he was hardworking, disciplined, and driven to succeed. The customer returned a few weeks later to have his car serviced. This time, I noticed him. Because his car was being serviced, he needed a lift home. Having developed a bit of style by this time, I put on my chic off-white trench coat and gave him a ride. His name was Wiland Knebel.

Wiland was born on June 25, 1939, in Breslau. At his birth, Wiland's mother was optimistic about his prospects in life; he had been born on a Sunday, which was considered lucky in Germany. He was the third of four children and had two brothers and a sister. When Wiland was a small child, his father purchased a bankrupt sawmill in Hultschin, which was about one hundred miles southeast of Breslau. At the time, Hultschin fell within German borders. The town is now known as Hlučín and is located in the Moravian-Silesian Region of the Czech Republic. Wiland and his family relocated to Hultschin so that his father could be closer to his business. In Hultschin, the Knebels lived a comfortable life due to the success of the factory.

Their success, however, was only short-lived. During the course of 1944, the Soviet offensive made major strides in the Eastern Front, advancing through the Ukraine, Estonia, Poland, and

Hungary. In February 1945, the Soviet army lay siege to Breslau and quickly progressed to Hultschin. They soon encircled the area. The Knebels's only hope was to gather what few possessions they could carry and flee through a small corridor that led west through Czechoslovakia. The winter was particularly brutal that year, and the refugees were forced to fight the elements as they attempted to make their way to safety. On numerous occasions, the refugees were forced to throw themselves onto the ground as low-flying Soviet aircraft on the attack suddenly swarmed the skies.

Wiland and his family were initially fortunate to secure passage on one of a number of German Air Force trucks that had been commandeered to transport refugees. The trucks also transported Wehrmacht soldiers who were abandoning their positions because there was nothing left to defend. But partway into their journey, advancing Russian ground forces, caught up and pushed all local moving vehicles either on to the side of the road or into a ditch so that they could pass through. Members of the Czech militia checked every truck. When the Russian soldiers reached the truck in which the Knebels were traveling, they questioned Wiland's father. His father spoke several languages, including a bit of Russian. The Russians inquired whether he was able to drive or not. Although he did know how to drive, he stated that he could not. His answer may have saved his life. Some of the men who did profess to having driving skills were conscripted into serving the Russian army and were eventually sent to prison camps in Siberia. As the Czech soldiers searched the truck, they found a pistol that had belonged to a fleeing Wehrmacht private. The soldiers began to shout angrily. They forced everyone to get off the truck and threatened to execute the passengers because the soldiers suspected them of being partisans. The refugees were rounded up and sent to a camp in Czechoslovakia.

Over the next six months, the Knebels were sent to two different labor camps in Prague: Beroun, a town located in the Central Bohemian Region; and finally, Písek, a town in the South Bohemian Region. The Knebels spent the majority of the six months in Beroun. During the day, the women were sent to nearby hospitals to help care for wounded soldiers. The men worked in the fields, assisting with various agrarian tasks. In the evenings, the camp kept a strict curfew of eight o'clock. At that time, all rooms were locked. The six members of Wiland's family shared a single room with seven other people. A bucket in the middle of the room served as a toilet for all the occupants. At night, they slept in triple bunk beds. Because of the limited opportunities to bathe and poor conditions within the camp, the bodies of the children quickly became riddled with the bites of bedbugs, fleas, and lice. Bitter cold, hunger, and the flu were constant also companions for the Knebels and the other refugees.

In December 1945, the Knebels were given permission to leave the camps because the camp administrators could no longer feed families with so many dependents. Wiland and his family took a freight train to Germany, crossing the border at Hof, a town located in the northeastern corner of Bavaria. American forces greeted them with hot chocolate and donuts, which felt like a luxury after the meager rations they had had in the labor camps. They eventually went on to Stuttgart and then traveled nine miles southeast to the city of Esslingen. They then reached their final destination of Oberesslingen, a suburb of Esslingen, where Wiland's aunt lived.

The Knebels lived in Oberesslingen for the next five years. Wiland enjoyed the company of a cousin close to his age. Getting enough to eat was always a concern in the postwar years. The two boys would occasionally steal food from the fields of local farmers. Wiland's father was quick to discipline his son's wayward behavior.

He whipped him with the leather belt he used to sharpen his razor.

In 1950, when Wiland was ten and a half years old, he and his family moved to Klosterreichenbach, a village in the Northern Black Forest in Baden-Württemberg, Germany's third-largest state. Klosterreichenbach was located along the banks of the Murg River, a tributary of the Rhine River. The surrounding area was mountainous and covered in a blanket of dense and rich forestation. Even in the height of the Roman Ages, when expansion was the main focus of the empire, the terrain dissuaded Roman soldiers from making much effort to penetrate the locale. It was, however, an ideal location for the Benedictine Order to build a monastery centuries later in 1082. Today, it draws tourists who are eager to escape urban life for fresh, clean air. When the Knebels moved to Klosterreichenbach, it was so small that it did not have a high school. Wiland traveled to the next town every day to attend school. Because the Northern Black Forest fell within the French occupation zone, Wiland received foreign language instruction in French in school, studying the language for a combined total of six years.

In 1955, having finished high school at the tender age of fifteen, Wiland began to work for a wood veneers factory owned by a company called Danzer und Wessel in Reutlingen, a small city and manufacturing hub about fifty miles east of Klosterreichenbach. He remained there for six months. After that, Danzer und Wessel sent him away for an internship in Kehl, a town on the Rhine located directly opposite of the French city of Strasbourg. He was later sent to Montreuil-sous-Bois, a suburb just east of Paris. A French company called Société Parisienne, which had a factory in Montreuil-sous-Bois, dealt in French black walnut for Danzer und Wessel. Société Parisienne manufactured the wood into veneers and then exported it to Germany. The recipients at Danzer und Wessel were dismayed to find that the products coming across the border were made poorly, which hurt the business. Wiland was sent to supervise production and ensure the quality of the veneers that were manufactured.

In 1960, Danzer und Wessel acquired a half interest in General Woods and Veneers, a company located in Longueuil, a city that sits on the south shore of the Saint Lawrence River, directly across from Montreal. Because of his French language skills and experience working abroad, Danzer und Wessel's senior management thought that Wiland was the perfect candidate to assist with operations in Canada. He arrived in Longueuil in September 1960 and started his employment with General Woods and Veneers.

Two and a half years later, Wiland and I met due to his fateful purchase of a Porsche. He immediately struck me as serious, handsome, and as someone with good values. I was impressed with his matter-of-factness and how unpretentious he was despite his fiscal success. Our first date took place at an upscale restaurant in Montreal called the Candlelight Restaurant.

Once again, I wore my off-white trench coat. I had always liked trench coats because of how they showcased my figure. I had long hair at this point but always put it up either in a bun or a French twist. I went into the dinner feeling beautiful, charming, and eager to learn more about this man who had come into my life.

At the dinner, however, Wiland spoke very little. He was much quieter than other men I had met. I did my best to fill the air with light conversation, but he did not join me in my chatter. The few times he did speak, however, he made thoughtful and intelligent statements that intrigued me and made me want to get to know him better. I felt a strong connection to him. His taciturn qualities at the dinner, though, did worry me, and I was concerned that I had bored him. I finished the evening hoping to hear from him but uncertain if I had garnered his interest.

I later learned that Wiland was self-assured enough that he did not feel the need to make small talk. He preferred to wait until he could make a substantive remark than engage in carefree banter. Wiland was the rare individual who had the maturity and wisdom to realize the value in listening even though it is a skill that many CEOs, businessmen, educators, doctors, and others overlook. He also recognized that most people go through life wishing to be heard more. He saw that by listening instead of speaking, he was able to offer support and understanding to the person who was speaking. This quality helped make him successful in his professional life. Listening is particularly useful in the field of sales. It is powerful in building relationships and can make a client feel validated and respected.

I did hear from Wiland shortly after our first date. He invited me to join him and one of his brothers Reinhard, as well as a colleague from work Carlo on a trip out of town. We went swimming in a lake in the Laurentian Mountains, which was located just over fifty miles northeast of Montreal. I had also occasionally gone there with my sister and cousins for weekend trips.

At the end of our date, Wiland asked me to come to his apartment so that he could show me photos of his family. As he recounted stories about his childhood, he leaned in close to me. I could feel a pull toward him. He captivated me, and I was utterly attracted to him. But reminding myself of my principles, I resisted temptation and backed away. I could imagine my mother in her youth going into the apartments of the men she encountered. I did not want to face the same fate of having two illegitimate children from different fathers.

Shortly thereafter, Wiland requested that I accompany him to Germany to meet his mother. He offered to buy a ticket for me. His mother was now a widow—Wiland's father had passed away when he was nineteen—and still living in Klosterreichenbach. I declined, clinging on to my principles. He flew to Germany alone. After he left, something inside me told me that I had made the wrong choice. It was my intuition. The heart speaks a silent language of its own, and it compelled me to put my stubborn determination to hold on to my principles aside. By this point, Yvonne and Erik had met and gotten to know Wiland, as my mother had. Mama, who clearly had never adhered to traditional values, said that she would support me if I decided to go. Yvonne and Erik also had no objections. I packed a suitcase and followed Wiland to Europe.

This was the first time I had been back in Germany since leaving Berlin. But I did not go back to Berlin on this trip. Instead, I went directly to the Black Forest. Although I had been there as a child, seeing it through adult eyes made it feel new and fresh. It was very different from where I had grown up in Northern Germany. In Baden-Württemberg, the food, colloquialisms, and culture were novel for me. Wiland's mother lived in a small and charming house. She kept her home in an elegant manner and also maintained an attractive garden. I was immediately impressed. At night before she went to bed, she would set the table for the next morning using a beautiful set of blue and white china. I made mental notes of these thoughtful touches, and when I returned to Canada, I purchased a set of blue and white china for myself. To this day, I enjoy using blue and white china. I also adopted her practice of setting the breakfast table the night before, which I also continue today.

After our visit with his mother, Wiland took me to Sanary-sur-Mer, a romantic fishing village located between Marseille and Nice in Southeastern France. Known as the sunniest place in France, Sanary-sur-Mer features a beautiful coastline dotted with small beaches. Every morning, a small fleet of artisan fishermen sold their catch off traditional wooden fishing boats. Sanary-sur-Mer is also notable for its literary history. The British author Aldous Huxley wrote his most renowned work *Brave New* World there in 1931. His friend and fellow writer D. H. Lawrence visited him during his sojourn there. With the rise of Nazism in the early 1930s, a number of German writers and intellectuals left Germany and relocated to Sanary-sur-Mer. Notable figures included playwright Bertold Brecht, Nobel Prize laureate Thomas Mann, philosopher Ludwig Marcuse, and writer Arnold Zweig.

During our visit, we visited the beach, went for swims in the ocean, and enjoyed delicious meals. Wiland was quite a gourmet as a young man, and on that trip, he introduced me to delicacies, such as escargot. We spent many romantic evenings laughing, watching the tide ebb and flow along the shore, and strolling down Sanary-sur-Mer's charming streets. I realized during that time that I had fallen in love with Wiland. It was there that we consummated our relationship, and I lost my virginity.

But on the way back to Canada, the energy between us felt different. Wiland was unusually quiet, even for himself. I began to feel dismayed. As the flight continued, Wiland remained reserved. I was certain that our relationship was over. I had betrayed my principles to be with him, and now I was heading down the same path as my mother. I imagined myself pregnant and alone. I started contemplating how I would orient my life to accommodate my child. I thought about where we would live, how I would support us, and the ways I could provide him or her with a loving environment.

Soon after we arrived in Canada, Wiland broke his silence. It turned out that his lack of conversation and engagement on the trip back was a reflection of his nerves, not his love for me. He had decided to propose. I was utterly surprised. A feeling of bliss poured over me, and my worries dissipated. I immediately accepted.

We got married six months after we got engaged on December 5, 1964. Even though Wiland was not religious and had not been baptized, and my ties to the church were not strong, our ceremony took place in the United Church in Montreal. Thirty-five guests attended. I had found a used wedding gown that cost $75. It was a long-sleeved ball gown that featured a lace overlay on top of several layers of white tulle. A hoop at the bottom of the dress kept its expansive shape. The dress came with a delicate elbow-length veil, which I wore with a tiara. I sold my car and used the proceeds to purchase the dress and a few other items for the wedding.

Our reception was held at the Ramada Inn. Although it was not an expensive or luxurious wedding, we had live musical entertainment, which an old colleague of mine from VW Sales and Services provided. His name was Chuck, and he had worked as a private chauffeur of the owner of the business. Chuck had always had an affection for me. He often drove me to my weekend job as a switchboard operator and gave me lifts to Woolworths. He joked that I was his "little swinging chick." Chuck played in clubs with his band during the weekends. Even before I had a boyfriend, Chuck had said that when I got married, he and his band would perform at my wedding. He kept us entertained the entire evening as Wiland and I danced away into the next phase of our lives.

On a trip to Germany to meet Wiland's mother.

FROM RUBBLE TO CHAMPAGNE

In my secondhand wedding dress at the Ramada Inn. Wiland still fits into his tuxedo.

5

MARRIAGE, MOTHERHOOD, AND OUR AMERICAN DREAM

Year 1965–1977

From the beginning of our married life, Wiland demonstrated thoughtfulness and practicality. He sold the Porsche, which was an exciting car for a young single man, but not as sensible for a newly married man looking to provide. In its place, he bought a VW Bug.

Wiland found us our first home as a married couple, an apartment in Dorval, an on-island suburb of Montreal. Located in the western half of the island, locally referred to as "West Island,"

Dorval falls within the part of Montreal that is historically anglophone. French speakers usually choose to reside in the eastern portion of the island. Founded in 1667, Dorval is the oldest city in the West Island, and one of the oldest in Canada and North America. When we moved there, it had become a haven for middle-class families and the home of Montreal-Dorval International Airport, currently known as the Montreal-Pierre Elliott Trudeau International Airport. Our apartment was charming and located right on Lake Saint Louis. Thanks to Wiland's sense of responsibility and careful planning, we were able to start out with no debt and some savings in our accounts. He was even able to pay for the furniture in full.

Even though Wiland was only four years older than me, I felt that he was far ahead of me in both schooling and life experience. I marveled over his sophistication and ambition and adored him. In my eyes, he could do no wrong. I had made strides in embracing my own strengths over the years. But having been looked upon with such disdain as a child in Germany and having faced so many setbacks in my schooling and work experiences, I lacked confidence and self-assurance. He saw potential in me that I did not know that I had. Wiland lovingly offered himself to me as a mentor, eager to nurture my growth and to show me that I was capable of much more than I ever thought possible. I responded with enthusiasm. I finally had found someone who could respond to my lifelong desire to better myself. Wiland led me without making me feel unintelligent or inferior in any way. Instead, he always showed how much he respected and appreciated me and offered support, encouragement, and unconditional love.

One of his first suggestions was for me to take French language classes. Given that over 65 percent of Montreal's population spoke French and more than twenty percent of all Canadians were francophone, Wiland felt that studying French would both help me to broaden myself and allow me to better engage with the community around us. I had previously learned a little bit of French from interacting with customers when I worked at the Woolworth's lunch counter. Wiland enrolled me in private lessons at the Berlitz Language School.

But as it turned out, I became pregnant right as I was starting my classes. I felt nauseous all the time. It was so bad that, at times, I would have to stop on my way to my lessons in order to use an airsickness bag. Despite my discomfort, I continued to go to my classes. I wanted to learn as much as possible. I also did not want to disappoint my husband.

I continued to feel sick through seven months of my pregnancy. Because I was unable to keep much down, I had only gained thirteen and a half pounds at my heaviest point. Wiland's schedule with General Woods and Veneers was rigorous, and he traveled frequently. He always did his best to come home whenever possible to support me. At the time, there was little support in workplace culture for fathers to be involved with pregnancies. Furthermore, most men did not go into the delivery room with their wives when it came time for a baby's arrival. Wiland was traveling when my water broke, and I went into labor. He did his best to come home, but I ended up delivering the baby on my own. My childhood had taught me how to be strong in the face of adverse conditions, and I made it through the labor and birth. Our first child, a son, was born on September 2, 1965, weighing over eight pounds. Wiland arrived the next day.

As I held my new son in my arms, I was overcome with love and emotion. I looked over his tiny hands and feet and his pink and fleshy body. I ran my fingers over his buttery soft skin and stared at his sleepy countenance. In that moment, I finally understood Mama's fierce devotion to me and to Yvonne from a mother's perspective.

I named my son Nikolai Knebel. I took his name from Count Nikolai Ilyich Rostov, a character in Leo Tolstoy's *War and Peace*, one of my favorite books. In the novel, Nikolai gives up his studies at a university to serve his country in the fight against Napoleon and his French invading forces. A man of principle, he refuses to use his family contacts to improve his rank in the army. Despite various challenges he faces over the course of the novel, Nikolai ultimately has a happy life, marrying well and maintaining close ties to friends and family. I had also seen David Lean's masterpiece *Doctor Zhivago*, which had caused a sensation in the box office that year. Although I did not ultimately use one of the names from the film, it helped cultivate my affection for Russian names.

With an infant son and a comfortable apartment, many would have seen our lives as a victory for an immigrant couple who had both come from so little. But Wiland had always demonstrated a sharp business acumen and a savvy mind when it came to investments. He was eager, ambitious, and determined to look for the best opportunities for our family. Before our son's arrival, Wiland decided to buy four building lots as an investment. I have clear memories of him walking around in his camel hair coat inspecting the lots. As he made his way around the properties, my heart swelled with love and pride. In my view, he could do no wrong. I adored him.

Wiland used one of the lots to build a house for our family. We moved into it when Nikolai was a few months old. The home was located in Saint-Bruno-de-Montarville, an off-island suburb of Montreal. Saint-Bruno-de-Montarville is a predominantly French-speaking municipality and is popular in Montreal due to its access to Mont Saint-Bruno, a national park and popular ski facility. The location was particularly convenient for Wiland due to its close proximity with Longueuil.

The house was charming and built with fieldstone, which Wiland had insisted upon. It had a double garage with a heavy garage door that I had to pull up because we did not have an electric door. The house had a big kitchen, a living room with an attractive fireplace, a beautiful staircase with wrought iron railings, and three bedrooms. The pièce de résistance was its extraordinary garden, the first one I ever had. Wiland had known that I had dreamed of having a garden and surrounding myself with beauty. He arranged to have a thousand tulips planted for me. Many of the flowers were not a color I particularly liked. Wiland was always looking to stand out or do something unique, and he chose flowers of unusual colors, such as burgundy red. But despite the color palate, I still loved the garden. It was extraordinary for the girl who had grown up around rubble to now enjoy a thousand tulips. Every time I looked at the garden, I could feel my husband's love. Wiland also built a lovely patio area with flagstones, and there was a small wooded area in the back.

By the time Nikolai reached his second birthday, I was three months pregnant with my second child. Once again, I fought nausea for seven months and only gained thirteen and a half pounds. Wiland was eager to come home more often to support me during my pregnancy, but his boss was callous and cared far more about business dealings than his employee's happiness. He criticized Wiland for coming home too often and put him on a schedule where he would be away for two weeks at a time and home only every other weekend.

Once again, Wiland was away when I gave birth, so I was alone on February 26, 1968, when our daughter arrived in the world. I tried not to think much about his absence but could not help but feel lonely. She had been born on a Monday, but Wiland was unable to join us until late on Friday of that week. After the weekend, he had to go away again.

Like her brother, my daughter, Tanya, was a robust baby and weighed over eight pounds. I once again turned to *War and Peace* and *Doctor Zhivago* to choose a name. Tolstoy had partially based Countess Natalya "Natasha" Ilyinichna Rostova, arguably the embodiment of the author's ideal woman, on his sister-in-law, Tanya Behrs. In *Doctor Zhivago*, KGB Lieutenant General Yevgraf Andreyevich Zhivago believes that Tanya Komarova is the long-lost daughter of his half brother, Doctor Yuri Andreyevich Zhivago and Lara Antipova. He tells her the story of her parents' ill-fated love affair. The name was beautiful and romantic.

I was now mostly alone with two young children. We did visit my mother, who lived only twenty minutes away often, and she was a great help with the children. But I remember pushing the baby carriage along and thinking, "Is this all there is?" I adored my children and treasured their presence in my life but had never felt more alone.

Wiland grew frustrated at the increasing demands of his job, which only took him away from us more frequently as his responsibilities grew. He had met another German immigrant named Manfred Böhlke, who was also in the wood industry. Manfred's business, Böhlke

Veneers, was based in Cincinnati. Wiland soon decided to purchase shares in the company and to partner with Manfred. Wiland sold our home, and in June 1968, when Tanya was three months old, we left Canada and moved to Ohio.

Although I trusted Wiland's judgment without question or reservation, I was dismayed that moving to Ohio meant giving up the beautiful house he had built. Even worse, our new home was an apartment. I did not like the idea of having to move into an apartment again. It felt like a significant step-down. I especially missed having a garden. I longed to have earth under my feet. But Wiland explained that even after selling our house, he needed to keep some finances available to invest in the new business he had joined. I agreed with his decision and was willing to make the sacrifice.

The apartment was located on Vienna Woods Drive in Cincinnati's Westwood neighborhood. Once one of Cincinnati's most desirable and elite neighborhoods, many of the city's industrial magnates, including Procter & Gamble, founder James Gamble, had built their estates in Westwood in the late nineteenth century. Overtime, an influx of German immigrants began to build a mix of apartments and houses in the area and working-class families began to move there.

After eighteen months in the apartment, our finances were again in a place where we could afford a home. In 1970, we rented a house on Kenwood Hills Drive in Madeira, a small and charming suburb of Cincinnati. Madeira's most renowned citizen was Clarence Harrison DeMar, who won the famed Boston Marathon seven times between 1911 and 1930.

In 1971, we bought the same house that we had rented and put it through an extensive remodeling process. We made so many changes that it was not recognizable by the time we finished. We added new floors, a new roof, beautiful arches, and more attractive windows. As a crowning glory, we dug a swimming pool into the backyard. Always looking for an investment opportunity, Wiland decided to buy the house across the street and rented it out for income.

The following year, in 1972, Wiland decided that it was time for him to set up his own business, the Knebel Export Company. After so many years in the wood industry, he had a deep understanding of how it worked and was confident in his ability to navigate the field. In the beginning, starting a business was stressful for Wiland. Building and maintaining a new business involves a constant struggle between uncertainty and determination. It often requires accepting prolonged periods of risk, trying to make good decisions in the always-changing market conditions, making mistakes, dealing with agreements that fall through, and sometimes weathering losses. It involves embracing apprehension over when success will come. Fortunately, Wiland had many of the qualities that are important in leading a new enterprise. He was always proactive in finding pragmatic solutions to any problems his clients raised. He never shied away from responsibility and held himself to high standards. Although he pressed hard to make smart deals, Wiland always demonstrated integrity and honesty, which garnered his clients' respect and loyalty. As a result, he drew customers from all over the world, including Germany, Switzerland, the Netherlands, Belgium, and Japan.

I was eager to play my role in supporting Wiland in his efforts. I became an excellent unofficial secretary for the business. I kept a pen and a pad of paper by the phone and was always ready to take messages properly and efficiently from clients. I also started to entertain customers on a regular basis. Often, they would come to our home unannounced, and I would need to provide a positive experience for them at the spur of the moment. This never fazed me because I made certain every day that the house was well maintained and ready for guests. My instincts for customer service from my days at Woolworths had been well-honed. When customers did come by,

I was able to set an elegant table quickly so that they could immediately sit down and relax. I had also become a good cook by this time and would make great efforts to prepare dishes that they would enjoy. Among my specialties were braised meats, cabbage, and dumplings. I often made steaks outside on the grill. I also enjoyed making *Rouladen*, a traditional German dish comprised of thin slices of meat stuffed with bacon, gherkins, and onions. The customers would often linger long after dinner was finished in order to talk shop over drinks. I would force myself to stay alert and participate. I quickly gained a lot of knowledge about the business through the many dinners I facilitated. Overtime, many of the customers came to know and like me. On numerous occasions, I heard them comment, "The sun is always shining at the Knebel house." The harmony between Wiland and me was always apparent. I did my best to play the gracious host and to offer my assistance to my husband, and I know that he was proud of me.

Another key component in Wiland's success was that he had a talent for identifying and connecting with other smart, ambitious people. These relationships are not only vital to doing well in a business but can also infuse fresh energy, inspiration, and clarity into one's goals. Very rarely, perhaps only once in the span of a long career, it is possible to find someone with whom there is the potential for even more than a business relationship. There is a soul connection. In 1972, on a fateful day, while playing a match at the tennis club, to which we belonged, Wiland met a fellow German immigrant named Karsten Joehnk. From that moment on, our lives were changed.

Karsten was born on August 11, 1935, in Hamburg, Germany. Like us, he grew up humbly, his childhood dominated by war. Before the rise of the Nazi Party, Hamburg had been an idyllic city, often described as the Venice of the north. Numerous canals and waterways crisscrossed the city, made accessible by nearly 2,500 bridges.

Connected to the North Sea by the Elbe River, Hamburg was home to Germany's largest port. The year before Karsten was born, Hamburg was named a *Gau* or de facto main administrative division of Nazi Germany. In 1937, Hitler declared that Hamburg was Germany's "Gateway to the World" and decided that it would be converted into a *Führerstädte*, or Führer city. At the advent of the war, Hamburg had had one of the largest concentrations of Jews in Germany. Starting in 1941, with the establishment of the Neuengamme concentration camp sixteen miles outside the city, Jewish families were marched into trucks and taken away, never to return. Two and a half weeks before Karsten's eighth birthday, on July 24, 1943, the British Royal Air Force and the United States Army Air Forces launched Operation Gomorrah, a campaign of air raids. Lasting for eight days and seven nights at the time, Operation Gomorrah was the heaviest assault in the history of aerial warfare. The constant bombings, dry conditions, and unusually warm weather created a vortex and whirling updraft of superheated air, which quickly turned into a tornado of fire, reaching a height of over 1,500 feet. The firestorm killed 42,600 civilians and wounded an additional 37,000. Surrounded by the dead and dying, Karsten watched as his city was virtually destroyed. British officials would later call the event the Hiroshima of Germany.

Fortunately, Karsten was a survivor. After the war, Karsten's family was assigned a basement apartment in one of the few buildings that remained in the city. As he watched his city rebuild under the auspices of British occupying forces, Karsten dreamed of a better life. He began his career working as a customs officer at the German border. Later, like so many immigrants before and after him, he decided to pursue a new life in the United States. But his hard times were not behind him. After settling in La Jolla, California, Karsten decided to travel home to Germany to visit his family. When he arrived, his father was in the hospital. His father had spiraled down into depression after getting diagnosed with prostate cancer after the war and had struggled for years. It eventually became too much for him, and he overdosed on pills. Karsten's father was taken to the hospital where his stomach was pumped. Later that day, Karsten decided to leave the hospital for a short time to get some fresh air. When he returned, his mother met him with a grim look on her face. "Now I am a widow," she declared.

Karsten returned to California, determined to make the most of his circumstances. Having witnessed devastation and tragedy from a young age, he had learned to soldier on even in the darkest of moments. He used that resilience to help him move forward from the loss of his father.

A few years later, Karsten learned about a Porsche-Audi dealership that had come up for sale in Cincinnati. He decided to take a chance and pursue the opportunity to own a business. Karsten was a visionary. Although it may be an unusual way to describe someone, Wiland and

I have commented on numerous occasions over the years how Karsten reminds us of a badger. Like a badger, Karsten has endless amounts of determination and persists in his efforts regardless of the challenges that come his way. He knows that success does not always come easily. Karsten also demonstrates the resourcefulness of a badger. When one approach fails, badgers try different methods until they find one that works. We noticed these qualities in Karsten from the beginning.

Wiland and I also immediately felt a heart connection with Karsten. The three of us understood each other as fellow children of war. We had all started our lives as the world around us was falling apart. We respected and related to the inner strength and fighting spirit Karsten had developed. Over time, I began to feel that Karsten was the male version of me, rising up from the rubble through sheer grit. Needless to say, Wiland and I now consider Karsten our dearest friend and a member of our family. We trust him completely and see him as one of life's greatest blessings.

With this special bond between us, we did not hesitate when Karsten approached Wiland in 1974 with a high-risk proposal. After several years of living in Cincinnati and struggling at the dealership, Karsten became discouraged and realized that it was not the best use of his talents. He decided to leave the industry and Ohio and to return to La Jolla, California, to pursue real estate. In launching his new venture, he had obtained a real estate broker's license. Karsten asked Wiland whether or not he would invest with him in apartments. The two men sat in a booth in a Howard Johnson restaurant and figured out the details of their arrangement on a paper napkin. Signing onto the agreement required great faith on Wiland's part because the possibility of a heavy loss was high. But if you give no trust, you will get no trust. Indeed, it is the willingness to take a leap of faith that gives you wings.

Karsten returned to La Jolla. He would contact Wiland whenever he found a suitable property. Wiland's confidence in Karsten was so great that he would wire the money without even seeing it. They started by purchasing eight units and then moved on to twelve. As Karsten identified more properties, they added to their portfolio. I did not worry. He had told me that he could still provide for me and our children even if we took a loss. He had been so prudent in saving that he was confident that we would not even have to alter our lifestyle if that happened. But I did not even need his assurances. I had never stopped Wiland from pursuing any opportunity. I believed so much in him that he could not do wrong in my eyes. In the end, the dealings with Karsten were a great success due to the hard work and foresight of two men I love and adore.

By this point, our son and daughter were no longer babies but young children with distinct personalities, preferences, and interests. They were both outgoing, active, and had cheerful dispositions. They were also adorable, with warm smiles, shining blue eyes, and soft blond hair. Watching them play or go for a swim in the pool, I sometimes thought about how when I was their age, I never could have imagined having such a life. I was grateful that they were growing up in a home with two devoted parents and that they never had to become familiar with hunger the way I had. I had a close relationship with my children and doted upon them as their mother, but I was also strict because I wanted to maintain order. I insisted that they come in from playing in the backyard at a certain time, their homework had to be complete and done well, and they had to listen to my authority. I used the kitchen spoon on their hands when they were misbehaving. Wiland was a wonderful and engaged father. Although his own father had whipped him, he chose not to follow in his father's footsteps. He never laid a hand on our children.

It was important to me to speak German with Nikolai and Tanya. I spoke to them exclusively in the language and would write our dinner menu in German on a blackboard in the kitchen every evening. On occasion, Nikolai would rebelliously stand in front of me, stomp his foot, and start speaking English with me. I would then firmly respond that he had to speak German in the house. He would put down his foot again and say, "I wish there was no such thing as German!" But I persisted. Now they both speak fluently and are grateful that I was strict about it. The irony is not lost on me that I was so insistent on promoting German language and culture in our home even though as a child, I had been denied German nationality and deemed stateless. Germany would not even accept me.

VIVIANNE KNEBEL

My firstborn son, Nikolai, at the age of five years old on an overseas cruise from New York to Hamburg. The ship was called the Hamburg. *It was brand new, and at the time, very luxurious.*

FROM RUBBLE TO CHAMPAGNE

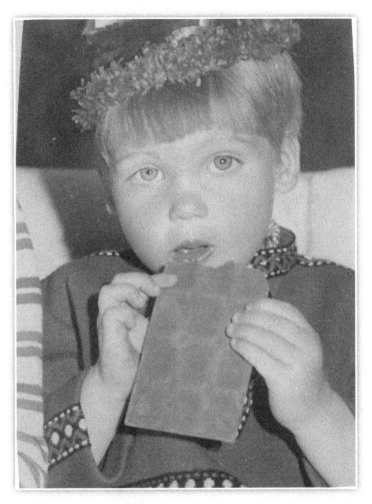

My daughter Tanya at the age of three years old. I had not tasted chocolate at her age—she has the whole bar!

Karsten and Wiland at our garden party.

6

COMING INTO MY OWN

Year 1978–2012

As our marriage entered into its second decade, Wiland continued to support me in my journey toward self-actualization. With each year, I became more aware of myself and my abilities. Having observed how well I had engaged in building relations with his clients and my hard work as a mother, among my other accomplishments, Wiland believed in me unfalteringly. But he still saw in me a reserve of untapped potential, and he urged me to go further. He constantly said to me, "You can do more. You are capable of more." He knew that I still questioned myself and lacked self-confidence, and he believed that this was holding me back. One of my better qualities is that I have always leaned toward those who know better than I do. I trusted Wiland wholeheartedly to lead me.

In 1978, an opportunity for growth came to me from a surprising source: aviation. Wiland often had to travel to locations that were far from major airports, and he thought that it would be much more convenient if he bought a small plane for his company. He suggested that I take flying lessons so that I could fly the plane myself. This was not a pursuit I had ever imagined taking up. I was full of doubt over whether I could do it. I also did not see myself as technically inclined, which I was certain was a necessary qualification for serving as a pilot. But Wiland was persistent. He assured me that I could do it. Wiland was not someone who offered compliments to be kind. He only said something encouraging when he truly meant it. Whenever Wiland believed in me,

I knew I could do it. I put my faith that whatever he suggested was right for me.

I started to take lessons. I began to familiarize myself with the different parts of the plane, such as the wings, ailerons, navigation system, communication system, fuel system, and engine. I learned how to create an accurate flight log, communicate effectively with maintenance and ground personnel, and how to plan a flight. My instructors also taught me some of the physics of flight, such as the Bernoulli principle, which explains how different air pressure flows around an airplane wing to cause lift. I studied how to keep an airplane balanced during flight and how the weight of passengers, cargo, or fuel can affect performance. Weather conditions can greatly affect a flight, so I developed a mastery of how to navigate in different weather phenomena. Finally, I learned how to maneuver an aircraft, including taking off, following airport traffic patterns, climbing, flying straight and making turns, coping with wind and turbulence, and how to land.

In total, I took thirty-nine lessons and performed six solo flights, something that seemed impossible at first. Through my training, I honed my skills of preparedness, staying calm under pressure, and handling unpredictable challenges. I did not enjoy flying and felt tense and stressed while doing so. But the feeling of accomplishment was incredible. I did not continue to fly after my sixth solo flight because Wiland changed his mind about purchasing a plane, and there was no longer a need for me to get my license. Nonetheless, I emerged from the experience with a new level of confidence and self-awareness. I now knew that I could step outside my comfort zone and excel.

Two years later, in 1980, I embarked upon a new challenge. Wiland had always enjoyed playing and following sports. As a young man in Germany, he had developed a love for soccer and had enjoyed watching professional matches. He had also played for a recreational team in Kehl. In the United States, Wiland expanded his interest to other sports. He started playing tennis and biking. In 1977, Jim Fixx's *The Complete Book of Running* became a national best seller. Fixx was largely responsible for popularizing the sport of running and extolling its virtues on physical and psychological health. Fixx had started running at the age of thirty-five when he weighed 214 pounds and smoked two packs of cigarettes per day. Through running, he lost sixty pounds and found the self-discipline to stop smoking. Wiland found Fixx's book so fascinating that he started running. He quickly developed a passion for it. I decided that I should try running myself. I asked Wiland whether he thought I could run a marathon. His eyes immediately lit up.

Running was not an activity that had ever appealed to me. I considered myself a stylish woman and liked wearing tailored dresses and high heels, not T-shirts and sneakers. But Wiland was so excited that I let him coach me for the race. Wiland was an excellent coach. He carefully devised a running program for me that involved six days of training each week followed by one rest day. We started my training regimen in the beginning of 1980 and set our sights on the Honolulu Marathon, which would take place in December of that year. I ran many of the same streets that DeMar had run on so many years before. I felt like I accomplished something every time I trained. I did not particularly enjoy running but relished the sense of achievement. I also loved that it made Wiland so happy. During my training, Wiland sometimes ran with me, but I also liked the solitude of running alone. I liked the feeling of having space for my own thoughts as my feet hit the pavement.

At the end of the year, Wiland and I set out for Hawaii. The Honolulu Marathon is considered a moderately challenging course because its temperatures vary from sixty-five degrees Fahrenheit to eighty degrees Fahrenheit, and it is relatively hilly compared with other marathons.

It starts near Ala Moana Beach Park, and among its highlights are downtown Honolulu, Diamond Head, Hawaii Kai, and its finish line in Waikiki's Kapiolani Park. If Wiland had not trained me so carefully, I would have been tempted to go out fast, which inevitably would have led me to run out of energy and not finish the race. But from the starting line, I had Wiland's strategy ingrained in my mind. I started slowly and holding myself back so that I could preserve my energy. Whenever I got tired, I focused simply on putting one foot in front of the other. I got into a rhythm and made sure to stay with it. As I got toward the end of the race and exhaustion set in, I focused on passing one person at a time. I ultimately finished all 26.2 miles in three hours and fifty-eight minutes. In 2016, when marathon times had gotten considerably faster due to improved training techniques and better running gear than when I ran thirty-six years before, *Running USA* found that the median marathon finishing time for women was four hours and forty-seven minutes. The median finishing time for men in 2016 was four hours and twenty-two minutes. I realized as I crossed the finish line that I was capable of more than I had ever imagined.

Wiland had told me that if I managed to finish the race in under four hours that he would buy me my dream home. He was so proud of me that he followed up on his promise. In 1982, we moved to Indian Hill, a posh suburb of Cincinnati, Ohio. It was the home of many of Cincinnati's luminaries, including Neil Armstrong, the American astronaut and the first person to walk on the moon; Robert A. Taft, son of President William Howard Taft and a presidential hopeful himself; and Peter Frampton, the rock musician, singer, and songwriter. Our new home was an old Tudor built in 1938. It was perched on a hill on a sprawling two-acre lot and featured a beautiful view. We added new windows and a wonderful Roman pool.

In 1984, Wiland suffered a small setback when he ruptured a disk in his back. He had to go to the hospital for surgery. With my newfound confidence, I felt capable of ensuring that his business would run smoothly in his absence. When a customer called with a concern, I drove him to show him samples of the wood products in which he was interested and expertly explained the wares to him. I also made certain to be by my husband's side as much as possible to ensure a healthy recovery.

By 1993, Wiland was growing weary of the wood industry. His business was not going as well as it had in the past, partially due to the loss of his best customer, who had passed away. He told me that he could continue on with his company but did not think that it was a worthwhile venture any longer. At the age of fifty-four, he had enough savings that he could afford to retire. I agreed that it was time and suggested that we leave Ohio and move to La Jolla, California.

From the time we had first gone into business with Karsten, we had visited him in La Jolla every year. Wiland had continued to invest with

Karsten. One property led to another, and the two men saw much success in their partnership. By the time Wiland retired, they co-owned three large apartment buildings and other properties in La Jolla and San Diego. Karsten had taught us that in real estate, it is important to live close to your holdings. With Karsten in La Jolla all those years, we were able to remain in Ohio without worry, but we felt that it was time to join him. Karsten found us our new home himself. We still live there today. It is a 2,800-foot Spanish house built in 1928, located only half a mile from the beach. It is set back from the street and features a gorgeous garden in the front with an iron gate and large hedge around it. In the back, there are lovely terraces.

I enthusiastically welcomed the change from Cincinnati to La Jolla. La Jolla is an affluent seaside community located twelve miles north of San Diego. It is surrounded by ocean bluffs and beaches on three sides. I was immediately drawn to the diversity of people, its temperate climate, and the gorgeous vistas it afforded from all its hills. The first time I went shopping, I went to the flower shop and left with my arms full of fresh flowers. As I took in the wonderfully intoxicating scent of the flowers, I said to myself, "Yes, I want to be here." I knew in that moment that it was a place where I would thrive.

The following year, in 1994, Wiland and I took a big step in our lives and became citizens of the United States. After moving to Canada, I had finally gained a nationality when I became a Canadian citizen. But becoming a United States citizen was far more meaningful to me. During my naturalization ceremony, as I listened to the speakers welcome me to my new status as a citizen, I became emotional. I had chosen to become a citizen of the United States and the country had chosen to accept me. I had never felt that sense of belonging before. I have come to see the United States as an extraordinary country. It is a place where people can truly aspire toward their potential, taking risks can lead to big payoffs, hard work and determination are rewarded, and possibilities are abundant if you are willing to go after them. In my experience, Americans are brave and openhearted. I feel that I can be who I am in the United States. There is no place where Wiland and I would rather live. I owe a lot to my adopted homeland, and I am truly grateful to it.

Even as we embraced our new lives as United States citizens, we never forgot my family in Canada. Mama, Yvonne and Erik and Datschi had all relocated to Toronto in the early 1970s. Wiland and I visited them every year, and thanks to Wiland's generosity, my mother came to La Jolla twice a year. We also invited my sister and brother-in-law to California many times. I made sure to stay in close touch with all of them.

In 1996, Mama experienced the final romantic chapter of her life. Georg had passed away that year. Although we were never close to him, Yvonne and I had come to accept him and appreciate the positive aspects of his presence in our lives. We chose to feel gratitude for his efforts to provide for us and keep a roof over our heads. Although he was Mama's husband, she had never had the passionate connection with him that she had shared with Valentino, the Spanish consul she had loved so long ago. That year, she and Valentino got back into contact after decades of silence. His own wife had sadly been committed to a mental institution, and he had never forgotten about Mama. The long-lost lovers made plans to meet again in Europe. Valentino spoke with Yvonne and asked whether Mama was still able to walk and if she was in good health. Yvonne reassured him that Mama was fit to travel and volunteered to accompany her. But just as Mama and Yvonne were getting ready to leave, they received the heartbreaking news that Valentino had passed away. As tragic as it was, I was still grateful that Mama knew that he had never stopped loving her.

In 2000, at the age of ninety, Mama fell ill herself. She had planned to come and visit me the following month, but then she called and said she was not well enough to come. I decided to go and see her. I did not think that she was at the end of her life, but I still felt a strong and urgent need to go to her. When I arrived in Toronto, she was moving about her apartment as usual. But the next day, she did not get out of bed. She never got out of her bed again. I stayed for two weeks and took care of her. I cleaned her apartment, baked cakes, and brought meal trays to her bedside several times a day. One day, she noticed a photo of her and me on the nightstand. It had been taken when we went on vacation to Hawaii. She reminisced about the trip and said how grateful she was that she got to share that time with me and how much she appreciated Wiland for making it possible. I crawled into bed with her, stroked her back, and tried to breathe her in. I knew in that moment that she was reaching the end of her days, but I could not grasp the finality of it.

At the end of the two weeks, I asked the social worker who had been assigned to my mother how long Mama had left. She responded that it could be weeks or months, but she and the doctors could not tell for certain. I gently told Mama that I would come back. At that point, she was losing her lucidity. She peered up at me. As I looked into her eyes, I saw just how piercingly blue they were. I said, "Mama, do you love me?" She nodded and gave me a kiss on the mouth. I got up to leave but turned around one last time and looked at her lying on the bed. I sobbed during the entire flight back to California.

When I got home, Wiland held me as I continued to cry. He told me that I should return to be with my mother and that he would come with me. We went back the next day. She passed away two days later. As she took her final breaths, I told my mother again and again that she could let go. "I'll come too," I said. Yvonne was surprised when she heard my words. She asked me how I could say that to Mama. I explained that I did not mean that I was going to die myself right then, but that I would always be with her. It did not matter if one of us was alive and the other had passed away. The bond between us did not depend on life.

My mother finally closed her eyes for the last time. Her legacy was one of unwavering and inexhaustible love and boundless compassion. She danced through life to her own choreography and refused to bend or give in to authorities or social norms. This choice made life difficult for her, but it was true to who she was. I believe that enabled her to experience the wonder of life and feel what touched her soul without judgment. She also had the rare ability to be utterly present in the moment. Mama could sit still for hours and just think. I would inquire, "Mama, isn't this terribly boring for you?" With a twinkle in her eye, she would retort, "You don't know what I am thinking about."

When my mother passed, my niece, Jessica, cut off a lock of Mama's hair, which I put into a little box. For a long time after she passed, I took that lock and pressed it against my face. I had a hard time letting go. Datschi told me it was obvious that I was always the one who needed the love of a mother the most. But in the years since losing her, I have found peace with her absence. I can still feel the impact she had on my life every day. Her presence is still within me.

But just as one life ends, another one begins. This is the natural order of life. Shortly before Mama passed away, I became a grandmother for the first time when Nikolai and his wife, Maria, had their first child, a son named Justin, on January 23, 2000. Nearly three years later, Nikolai and Maria welcomed a daughter, Natalie, on December 10, 2002. Tanya and her husband, Iain, brought their son, William, into the world on April 30, 2003. A daughter, Lilias, followed on March 8, 2005. I have a close and loving relationship with my children and grandchildren. When my children got married, I gained another son and a daughter. My children have always been honest with me. Tanya told me in recent years that I often came across as rigid when she was growing up. I have taken her critique to heart and worked on loosening up.

In 2002, Wiland and I traveled to Berlin along with his brother and sister-in-law. It was the first time I had been back there since leaving as a child. I remembered how when I left as a thirteen-year-old girl, I had imagined returning as a refined and elegant woman. As I walked around the streets of Berlin in my fashionable clothing with my husband by my side, people gave me looks of admiration and respect. When I had left, I had lived in government-subsidized housing. But now, Wiland and I were able to stay in, one of the city's elite hotels. One evening, as I sat in the luxurious surroundings of the hotel listening to beautiful music, I could not help but think of Mama. I had brought an Indian coin ring she had left to me along on the trip and wore it even though it was too large for my finger. A waiter brought us two flutes of champagne. I tapped the ring on the champagne glass and said, "Mama, we are back."

During our visit, I took Wiland, his brother, and his sister-in-law to see the apartment building where I had lived. The same janitor who had worked there when I was a child was still living there. Her name was Frau Geisler. She remembered that my mother had always dressed me in short skirts because she did not like the look of little girls in long skirts and miniskirts were in fashion. She commented that the skirt I wore that day was just as short as ever. The spirit of my younger self was still with me in some ways. As we crossed to do some shopping at the KaDeWe, where I had once begged for leftovers, I noticed a patch of grass. As a child, I passed that patch every day on my way home from school. I used to stop there and pick twenty or thirty *Gänseblümchen*, or little white lawn daisies, to make a small bouquet for my mother. Mama would then put the flowers in a small cup and tell me how much they delighted her, As Wiland and our other traveling companions patiently looked on, I revisited that moment of my youth. I bent down and started gathering the flowers. With a bouquet forming in my hands, I felt both sentimental for the past and triumphant in how far I had come.

Five years later, thanks once again to Wiland's generosity, I returned to Berlin another time with my sister. We stayed in the Hotel Kempinski Berlin Kurfürstendamm, also one of the city's most luxurious hotels. We revisited all the places that had figured into our childhood, including the bunker in the zoo where Mama had found shelter for us many times, the market where I collected discarded wooden crates, and the KaDeWe. At night, back in the comfort of our hotel, I ordered champagne, and we reminisced about the past.

One afternoon, as I crossed a street near the Kaiser Wilhelm Memorial Church, I suddenly felt unwell. In German, there is an expression, *"Jemandem ist eine Laus über die Leber gelaufen,"* or "A louse has walked over someone's liver." I could feel some negative energy in the air. I believe that energy remains in a place for a long time and can far outlast the people or events from which it originated. There may have been an air attack that impacted that street corner that was somehow embedded in my subconsciousness even though I would have been under two years old when the bombs fell. I had the same uncomfortable feeling when I was cleaning out some drawers in my mother's apartment after she passed away. I came across some old immigration photos of me and Georg. The energy felt so oppressive that I had to restrain myself from ripping them up. It was a reminder that the darkness of the past can still linger on.

During that trip, Yvonne and I made a special trip to the Kaiser Wilhelm Memorial Church. It was still in ruins when we left Berlin but had been rebuilt in the many years since then. The middle tower had been left as a war memorial. After the church had been bombed during the war, Mama had picked through the ruins and found a beautiful urn. As a little girl, I remembered her putting violets in there. When Mama passed away and was cremated, Yvonne had put her ashes in there. While searching through the ruins, Mama had also found beautiful tesserae from a mosaic that had been destroyed. They were pale turquoise, golden yellow, and dark blue. Mama had treasured the tesserae through the years and had brought them with us to Canada. Yvonne brought three of them with her to Berlin. We wanted to give a piece of our history back to the city. The administration of the church gladly accepted our gift and put them under a glass showcase so that worshippers and guests could all enjoy them. Before we left the church, Yvonne and I lit three candles, one for Mama and one for each of us. I looked over at my sister, the flame illuminating her beautiful face. The bond between us, which Mama had so lovingly fostered, was as strong as ever.

FROM RUBBLE TO CHAMPAGNE

Yvonne and me on our trip down memory lane in Berlin to bring back three mosaics to the Kaiser Wilhelm memorial church and light three candles.

7

THE MOST BEAUTIFUL TIME OF MY LIFE

Year 2013–

*W*hen I turned seventy in 2013, I became who I was always meant to be. I had bloomed into the person Wiland had always seen in me. I no longer wavered from insecurities or questioned my abilities. Instead, I became firm in my convictions and my sense of self.

My progress could not have come at a better time because that year, I faced one of my greatest challenges. A routine mammogram had revealed an abnormality that required further testing.

When the results came, I learned that I had cancer. As my doctor revealed the news, I was completely shocked. Blood rushed to my face. The doctor gave me a moment to catch my breath. She explained, "No one ever wants to hear the word, but if you are going to hear cancer, you want what you have." We had caught the cancer early at stage one. After my appointment, I called my daughter on the phone. When I shared the news, she immediately responded, "Oh, Mom," in the most loving and gentle voice. I immediately started to cry.

That night, I set the breakfast table as I always did. The next morning, I sat down and asked myself how I was going to handle having cancer. I decided that I would take as positive of an approach as possible. In that moment, I felt a shift inside me. I no longer felt like a victim. Instead, I felt grateful for early detection. I could tell that this crisis had already made me stronger. Looking back on my life, I could see how each crisis had prepared me even more for the next crisis. It was a reminder that within the brief span of life that we have, we each have the capacity within ourselves to take charge and to find beauty in it. I realized in that moment that my cancer diagnosis had brought me closer to my true, resilient self.

I started a regimen of radiation, anticancer pills, and regular doctor visits. I went through radiation five days a week for six weeks. During each session, I felt hopeful and upbeat. Life became more vivid and illuminated. I saw each day as another gift and every moment as special. Although others may have gone through the same set of circumstances full of despair, I chose to see things in a different light. Despite the initial shock, the prospect of death can be a great teacher in that you learn to make the most of your precious time. At the end of my treatment, the nurses hugged me and said they would miss my cheerfulness. I was now cancer-free and immensely grateful to be healthy.

Coping with breast cancer led me to become more connected with my spiritual path. Wayne Dyer, the American self-help author and a motivational speaker, played a pivotal role in my journey. In *Pulling Your Own Strings: Dynamic Techniques for Dealing with Other People and Living Your Life As You Choose,* Dyer explains how important it is to take control of one's life and not see oneself as a victim despite the numerous forces and factors that may convince you otherwise. He notes that the freest people are those who are firmly committed to their inner peace. They are the people who refuse to allow the whims and wills of others to define how they should live their lives and who they should be. Instead, they focus on their own choices without worrying about how others feel about them. Dyer helped me to recognize how much the vicissitudes of my early life had impacted me and depleted my strength. I realized that so much of my past suffering came from my sensitivity to everyone and everything around me. But there was always a choice. I just did not always see it. In facing cancer, I began to realize that although I could not control my illness, I did have complete authority over my response to it. I had chosen not to be a cancer victim but instead to fight the disease with positivity and hope.

It was during this time that I began to meditate. I realized that part of finding the freedom that Dyer had so fervently described was learning to separate myself from the pressures, expectations, and judgments that I encountered. I needed to burrow deep within myself and know who I was so that I could decide what was meaningful and worth listening to and what did not matter. By connecting with my true self, I could better face any challenge that came my way and deepen my appreciation of all life's glory.

I had initially tried meditation through sitting in silence, but to me, a minute of silence felt like an eternity. Within seconds, I felt that I could not last a moment longer. I became distracted by the noises around me, the discomfort I felt in my hips, the numbness starting to form in my legs, and the countless thoughts leaping about inside my mind. A year later, I tried a sound meditation Dyer had created and found it far more accessible. Having the support of guidance made all the difference for me.

For over five years, I have been meditating in the morning for forty-five minutes and in the evening for twenty minutes. When I meditate, I feel open to my center and feel close to myself. There is a sense of calm that comes over me. I am able to sweep away the cobwebs that fill up my mind. My thinking has become more acute; my will, stronger; my emotions, more sensitive; and above all, I experience more gratitude.

During my cancer treatment, I also came to appreciate poetry. It is the language of the heart. I enjoy reading the words of great thinkers and learning from their teachings. Poetry is also a vehicle through which I can experience the entire range of human experiences and emotions. It can extoll the greatest wisdom or poke fun at the sweet foolishness of life. Although I had always found beautiful words enchanting, I started finding comfort in poetry when I was a cancer patient. Poetry began to feel like food for my soul.

It was through poetry that I began to reconcile my feelings on life and death. One of my favorite Robert Frost poems is "The Secret Sits":

The Secret Sits

> We dance round in a ring and suppose,
> But the Secret sits in the middle and knows.

As I read these words, I thought about how we spend our lives dancing about in a circle. But it is in the center where God or "the Secret" sits. Only God knows what truly exists. It was liberating to realize that I did not and could not control all aspects of the world around me. I can only move about on this earth like all other human beings, accepting the great mystery that is the universe or God.

Poetry also has the power to create human values. As I went through radiation, I found *A Psalm of Life* by Henry Wadsworth Longfellow particularly inspiring. It reads in part:

A Psalm of Life

What The Heart Of The Young
   Man Said To The Psalmist.

Tell me not, in mournful
   numbers,
Life is but an empty dream!
For the soul is dead that
   slumbers,
And things are not what they
   seem.

Life is real! Life is earnest!

And the grave is not its goal;
Dust thou art, to dust returnest,
Was not spoken of the soul.

Not enjoyment, and not sorrow,
Is our destined end or way;
But to act, that each to-morrow
Find us farther than to-day…

Lives of great men all remind us
We can make our lives sublime,
And, departing, leave behind us
Footprints on the sands of time…

Let us, then, be up and doing,
With a heart for any fate;
Still achieving, still pursuing,
Learn to labor and to wait.

Here, the poet argues against the biblical treatise that human life is not important and that we are simply made of dust and will return to dust in the end. Instead, the poet is boldly optimistic. He celebrates human life and promotes the idea that through dedication and hard work, we can make lasting contributions. Longfellow's words inspire me to make the most of the life I have been given and to seek meaning in my experiences. It speaks to the work ethic that has driven me all my days and the eagerness I have to keep embracing opportunities to learn and grow.

Another source of inspiration is my garden, which has now become my sanctuary. The garden has been featured on the La Jolla Secret Garden Tour. I have created a color scheme of blue, white, and soft pink—all romantic colors—for the garden. I have bushes full of white camellias; red, pink, and white azaleas; blue lobelias; white alyssum; and pink bougainvillea. Trimmed boxwoods offer a sense of classic, clean order. The eucalyptus trees add softness and balance. A lot of the garden is form cut, but the trees add a degree of wildness. I also keep a small kitchen garden where I grow herbs and salad. Along one side of the garden is a white wall with a niche cut out of it where I keep a Buddha statue. The Buddha reminds me of stability, thinking good thoughts, and keeping my heart and mind pure. Even just glancing at the statue brings out peaceful feelings in me.

I feel most myself when I am gardening. When I dig, I always feel a powerful pull to get in touch with the earth. I make sure to place both hands in the soil and feel the wet and soft texture in between my fingers. Gardening also opens in me a space for expansive emotional discovery. When you garden, you transform a space and watch life take hold before your eyes. It feels miraculous that tiny hard seeds can grow into extraordinarily colorful flowers. Seeing this change makes me feel alive. When I am among the flowers, I am away from all that distracts me, and I feel like I can really hear myself and my thoughts. It centers me and grounds me. Every day, when I go into the garden with my cup of coffee and do the rounds,

I am immediately struck by how grateful I am to have it.

To me, nature is beauty in its rawest, most glorious, and most divine form. Beauty brings us closer to God; indeed, I feel closest to God in my garden. I have come to appreciate how beauty builds you up. The minute you look at something beautiful, you cannot have an unpleasant thought. Beauty is truth. It gives you strength. I have learned to build my surroundings in a way that gives me strength. For instance, if I set my table with beautiful flowers and green apples, then I derive strength from it.

On December 5, 2014, Wiland and I celebrated our 50th wedding anniversary. For the occasion, Wiland wrote this poem:

Wedding Anniversary

A half a century ago today, two
   young Germans became one
   behind a stack of hay!

Saving every penny, admired by many.
Discipline and hard labor the strength of this couple will be impossible to topple,
Unknown to both is the future, the remaining time shorter, but therefore even sweeter.
The ardent wish to stay happy and healthy will make them on December 5, 2014
Immensely more wealthy.

For us, our anniversary was more than a marking of the passage of time. It was a triumphant celebration of how far we had come in our lives together. We both also noted how our relationship had changed to accommodate the personal growth in me that Wiland had so lovingly fostered. Although he had initially played more of a leadership role in our relationship, there had been a shift. The teacher and student dynamic in our relationship had given way to one where we stood as equals. I had found my voice and my confidence. I could see and feel the change within me. I had become the person Wiland always knew me to be.

My journey toward self-discovery prepared me well for the next challenge Wiland and I faced. In late 2017, while playing tennis, Wiland experienced shortness of breath. He could not run to the ball as quickly as usual. He assumed that this was the result of getting older. Once again, a friendship played a major role in guiding us in the right direction. Wiland frequently played with Sheldon "Shel" Diller, a person of whom he thinks highly. Shel immediately suggested that Wiland see a doctor, but Wiland was stubborn and shrugged off the recommendation. He continued to ignore his symptoms. Fortunately, Shel cared about Wiland so much that he continued to push him to seek professional care. Finally, Wiland relented and saw a doctor. Shel had been right to show so much concern. Wiland immediately was sent to the operating room for open-heart surgery, four bypasses, and a heart valve repair. Shel's concern and persistence saved Wiland's life.

Learning of Wiland's heart condition was a great shock to me. Tanya had encouraged me to come to her home to have dinner after leaving the hospital. I was so distraught that I drove right by her house. I had seen Wiland right after he came out of surgery. The doctor had warned me that he would be disoriented or lethargic at best following the surgery, but I still wanted to see him. He was lying there like a stone. Under the heavy veil of anesthesia, he looked lifeless. In that moment, I thought that this was how a dead person looked. I stroked his head and gave him a kiss. Even though he could not hear me, I promised him that everything was going to be fine and that I would get him well.

Wiland spent two weeks in the hospital. Although some might find this surprising, I actually saw his recovery as a beautiful time. I had always had a strong, innate ability to nurture and felt my true self shine through as I tended to him. Wiland had always been so good to me, and I was grateful for the chance to give back to him. I nursed him back to health with every bit of love I had to offer. One of the nurses who came in regularly told me that I would have made a great nurse.

Impressionist painting in oil by impressionist painter Toni Williams (was done at the garden show of myself at my garden table on May 2018).

FROM RUBBLE TO CHAMPAGNE

(Front garden) Garden was featured in the La Jolla Secret Garden Tour.

Large terrace in the back of the house where we have had many family dinners.

FROM RUBBLE TO CHAMPAGNE

Small breakfast terrace in the back of the house.

I was determined to keep Wiland's spirits up as he healed. Because Wiland was so used to staying active, I was worried that he might become depressed. I did all that I could to create a warm and cheerful environment for him. I played Christmas music in his hospital room and kept an arrangement of oranges, marzipan, and nuts on the table. I prepared sandwiches in a charming way so that they resembled little tapas. Shel also came to the hospital at regular intervals to visit him. Due to my efforts and those of friends like Shel, Wiland did not become depressed. Instead, he and I became even closer. Love has so many facets, and nurturing someone through a hard time can truly reinforce and strengthen the feelings that first connected you. As Wiland came back to health, he and I saw that we could face anything together.

The challenges I have overcome over the years and the journey of growth I have taken have given me the ultimate gift: a profound sense of gratitude. It is now that character that best defines me. I have realized that there is always a place for gratitude. On the more expansive end of the spectrum, there are the people who come into your life and change it for the better, the opportunity to learn and progress, good health, and good fortune. Or you can feel gratitude for something as simple as the scent of a rose, the smile on a child's face, or a delicious meal. There is always something for which to be grateful. At the root of gratitude is paying attention. It involves noticing and giving thanks for all aspects of your life, from the mundane to the extraordinary. I have observed that through my gratitude practice, I have become happier and more fulfilled because I take note of and appreciate what I once took for granted.

Practicing gratitude has also been healing for me. I am certain that it played a significant role in helping me through my cancer treatment and supporting Wiland's recovery. The positivity and optimism I generated through my gratitude fueled me on difficult days. Gratitude has helped me to trust myself and my abilities even in moments of great uncertainty. I have also learned to acknowledge and accept painful moments. I realize that difficult moments can be instructive if you are willing to receive them as such. The lessons you encounter may not be pleasant, but they fortify you for the future. In addition, I have learned to block feelings of victimhood and any thoughts that are not loving. For example, if I am on a plane and there is a delay due to a mechanical failure, I feel grateful that the engineers working on the problem are keeping me safe. It is always possible to find good, even in chaos. You become strong as a result of your ability to find what is good in life. You are what you think.

Epilogue

*W*iland once told me that meeting me was like bending down to pick up a stone that looked different from all the others. After he polished it off, he found out that it was a diamond—strong, enduring, and shining. With all odds against me from the beginning of my life, I have emerged as an accomplished woman, completely fearless, with only love in my heart. As Wayne Dyer once explained, the most beautiful people have suffered, but the outcome is compassion, sensitivity, gentleness, and love. After a lifetime of searching and seeking, I have found myself. The dreams I manifested as a young girl have become reality and so much more.

Now in my seventies, I am in the most beautiful and fulfilling time in my life. I have become who I was meant to be. I have clarity, and I become more aware as I go through life. I listen closer, I observe with great attention, and I truly live. I am able to love myself now because I know myself inside. I am content with who I am. My life is joy and ecstasy. I have the peacefulness of a fully lived and appreciated life. I am far from stagnant; I am constantly at work on improving myself and developing further. Each day brings new treasures. I am now rich in every way. And my greatest wealth is that which comes from within.

Most people seem to fear aging. For me, the winter of my life has been its most extraordinary chapter. I have become aware that aging is not defined solely by the physical decay of the body but comes with gifts of great value. One of those gifts is the maturity not to stand in judgment but to approach the world through loving and wonder-struck eyes. For everything you lose, you gain something else. I have learned to say yes to whatever nature asks of me and not to fight situations that cannot be changed. I have thereby learned to avoid constant war with myself and my environment. I try to find my strengths and build on them.

Wiland and myself (taken January 2019)

At this stage of my life, I have no fear of death, which will eventually come, because I have truth, peace, and love, which are eternal. I have an extreme love and zest for life. The real me is invisible. It is the life force, love, and peace I carry. I believe that life force will remain even when I am gone, which is why I am at peace with death.

I have learned that you are not limited to your body. As Walt Whitman pointed out so well, no one can stop the natural course of the body. You live in a vessel that has an invisible future pull. It must go wherever nature takes it, and ultimately, it will reach its end. It is a temporary shelter for your soul throughout your life journey. When I was fourteen and fell into a deep meditative state, I recoiled in fear. But now, so many years later, I have an answer for what I experienced. I learned that the body and mind are separate. You are not just your mind but also exist in a realm beyond your mind. There is a system or intelligence that is the real you. You are part of the universe. Every leaf, every stone, and every flower are all a part of you. When you realize that everything is one, you have experienced your true nature. God is everywhere, and you are part of God.

There is still so much I want to do in my life, but all my prayers have been answered. I am blessed with a close-knit, loving family, including four beautiful grandchildren. I am most grateful to have Wiland by my side. He remains my rock to this day. He is the kindest human being and fulfills my every wish. We have now been married for fifty-four years and are moving together into a new stage of life. Our love will illuminate our path forward.

About the Author

$\mathcal{V}$ivianne Knebel was born illegitimate in 1943 in the epicenter of Nazi power, Berlin, Germany. Her free-spirited and strong-willed mother, Marija, fought to keep her alive among falling bombs and Soviet attacks. After the end of World War II, with much of Berlin razed to the ground, Vivianne came to know poverty and constant hunger. As a teenager, she immigrated to Canada, but in her new homeland, times became so desperate that she had to beg for money to eat. After dropping out of school to find work, Vivianne became the victim of sexual harassment. Spiraling into depression, she attempted to take her life, but was miraculously saved by a six-year-old child.

Falling in love with a fellow German immigrant, Wiland, proved a pivotal turning point for Vivianne. He saw a wellspring of potential in her and believed that she could become more than she had ever imagined. They married and moved to the United States. In the land where so many immigrant dreams are built, Wiland encouraged Vivianne to pursue endeavors that would test her mettle, including piloting a plane, running a marathon, and taking on a key role in supporting his business enterprise. Vivianne's journey of personal growth later gave her the courage to battle cancer and embrace a spiritual life.

Through hardship, demoralization, yearning, searching, loving, inspiration, and growth, Vivianne has discovered the ultimate secret to a life well lived: a grateful heart.

Notes

Notes

Notes

Notes

Notes

Notes

CPSIA information can be obtained
at www.ICGtesting.com
Printed in the USA
LVHW061300190922
728662LV00026B/186/J